questioning identity

AN INTRODUCTION TO THE SOCIAL SCIENCES: UNDERSTANDING SOCIAL CHANGE

This book is part of a series produced in association with The Open University. The complete list of books in the series is as follows:

Questioning Identity: Gender, Class, Ethnicity
edited by Kath Woodward

The Natural and the Social: Uncertainty, Risk, Change
edited by Steve Hinchliffe and Kath Woodward

Ordering Lives: Family, Work and Welfare
edited by Gordon Hughes and Ross Fergusson

A Globalizing World? Culture, Economics, Politics
edited by David Held

Knowledge and the Social Sciences: Theory, Method, Practice
edited by David Goldblatt

The books form part of the Open University courses DD100 and DD121/ DD122 *An Introduction to the Social Sciences: Understanding Social Change.* Details of these and other Open University courses can be obtained from the Course Information and Advice Centre, PO Box 724, The Open University, Milton Keynes MK7 6ZS, United Kingdom: tel. +44 (0)1908 653231, e-mail general-enquiries@open.ac.uk

Alternatively, you may visit the Open University website at http://www.open.ac.uk where you can learn more about the wide range of courses and packs offered at all levels by The Open University.

For availability of other course components visit the webshop at www.ouw.co.uk, or contact Open University Worldwide, Michael Young Building, Walton Hall, Milton Keynes MK7 6AA, United Kingdom for a brochure. tel. +44 (0)1908 858785; fax +44 (0)1908 858787; e-mail ouwenq@open.ac.uk

questioning identity:
gender, class, ethnicity

edited by kath woodward

London and New York

in association with

The Open
University

First published 2000 by Routledge; written and produced by The Open University
Second edition 2004
11 New Fetter Lane, London EC4P 4EE

Simultaneously published in the USA and Canada by Routledge
29 West 35th Street, New York, NY 10001

Routledge is an imprint of the Taylor & Francis Group

© 2000, 2004 The Open University

This text has been printed on paper produced in Sweden from wood from managed forests using an elemental chlorine-free bleaching process. It has been stated as being environmentally friendly by the Swedish Association for the Protection of Nature.

Edited, designed and typeset by The Open University.

Printed in the United Kingdom by The Bath Press, Bath.

British Library Cataloguing in Publication Data
A catalogue record for this book is available from The British Library

Library of Congress Cataloging in Publication Data
A catalogue record for this book has been requested

ISBN 0-415-32967-1 (hbk)

ISBN 0-415-32968-X (pbk)

ISBN 0-203-39213-2 (ebk)

2.1

Contents

The Open University course team

John Allen, *Professor of Geography*

Penny Bennett, *Editor*

Pam Berry, *Compositor*

Simon Bromley, *Senior Lecturer in Government*

Lydia Chant, *Course Manager*

Stephen Clift, *Editor*

Allan Cochrane, *Professor of Public Policy*

Lene Connolly, *Print Buying Controller*

Jonathan Davies, *Graphic Designer*

Graham Dawson, *Lecturer in Economics*

Ross Fergusson, *Staff Tutor in Social Policy*

Fran Ford, *Senior Course Co-ordination Secretary*

Ian Fribbance, *Staff Tutor in Economics*

David Goldblatt, *Co-Course Team Chair*

Richard Golden, *Production and Presentation Administrator*

Jenny Gove, *Lecturer in Psychology*

Peter Hamilton, *Lecturer in Sociology*

Celia Hart, *Picture Researcher*

David Held, *Professor of Politics and Sociology*

Susan Himmelweit, *Professor of Economics*

Stephen Hinchliffe, *Lecturer in Geography*

Wendy Hollway, *Professor of Psychology*

Gordon Hughes, *Senior Lecturer in Social Policy*

Wendy Humphreys, *Staff Tutor in Government*

Jonathan Hunt, *Co-publishing Advisor*

Christina Janoszka, *Course Manager*

Pat Jess, *Staff Tutor in Geography*

Bob Kelly, *Staff Tutor in Government*

Margaret Kiloh, *Staff Tutor in Social Policy*

Sylvia Lay-Flurrie, *Secretary*

Gail Lewis, *Senior Lecturer in Social Policy*

Siân Lewis, *Graphic Designer*

Liz McFall, *Lecturer in Sociology*

Tony McGrew, *Professor of International Relations, University of Southampton*

Hugh Mackay, *Staff Tutor in Sociology*

Maureen Mackintosh, *Professor of Economics*

Eugene McLaughlin, *Senior Lecturer in Criminology and Social Policy*

Andrew Metcalf, *Senior Producer, BBC*

Gerry Mooney, *Staff Tutor in Social Policy*

Lesley Moore, *Senior Course Co-ordination Secretary*

Ray Munns, *Graphic Artist*

Karim Murji, *Senior Lecturer in Sociology*

Sarah Neal, *Lecturer in Social Policy*

Kathy Pain, *Staff Tutor in Geography*

Clive Pearson, *Tutor Panel*

Ann Phoenix, *Professor of Psychology*

Lynn Poole, *Tutor Panel*

Raia Prokhovnik, *Senior Lecturer in Government*

Norma Sherratt, *Staff Tutor in Sociology*

Roberto Simonetti, *Lecturer in Economics*

Dick Skellington, *Project Officer*

Brenda Smith, *Staff Tutor in Psychology*

Mark Smith, *Senior Lecturer in Government*

Matt Staples, *Course Manager*

Grahame Thompson, *Professor of Political Economy*

Ken Thompson, *Professor of Sociology*

Diane Watson, *Staff Tutor in Sociology*

Stuart Watt, *Lecturer in Psychology*

Andy Whitehead, *Graphic Artist*

Kath Woodward, *Course Team Chair, Senior Lecturer in Sociology*

Chris Wooldridge, *Editor*

External Assessor

Nigel Thrift, *Professor of Geography, University of Oxford*

Series preface

Questioning Identity: Gender, Class, Ethnicity is the first in a series of five books, entitled *An Introduction to the Social Sciences: Understanding Social Change.* If the social sciences are to retain and extend their relevance in the twenty-first century there can be little doubt that they will have to help us understand social change. In the 1990s an introductory course to the social sciences would have looked completely different.

From a global perspective it appears that the pace of change is quickening, social and political ideas and institutions are under threat. The international landscape has changed; an intensification of technological change across computing, telecommunications, genetics and biotechnology present new political, cultural and moral dilemmas and opportunities. Real intimations of a global environmental crisis in the making have emerged. We are, it appears, living in an uncertain world. We are in new territory.

The same is also true of more local concerns. At the beginning of the twenty-first century both societies and the social sciences are in a state of flux. *Understanding Social Change* has been written at a moment that reflects, albeit in a partial way, subterranean shifts in the social and cultural character of the UK. Established social divisions and social identities of class, gender, ethnicity and nation are fragmenting and re-forming. Core institutions such as the family, work and welfare have become more diverse and complex. It is also a moment when significant processes of change have been set in train – such as constitutional reform and European economic and monetary union – whose longer-term trajectory remains uncertain. The flux in the social sciences has been tumultuous. Social change, uncertainty and diversity have rendered many of the most well-established frameworks in the social sciences of limited use and value. Social change on this scale demands fresh perspectives and new systems of explanation.

In this context *Understanding Social Change* is part of a bold and innovative educational project, for it attempts to capture and explore these processes of momentous social change and in doing so reasserts the utility and necessity of the social sciences. Each of the five books which make up the series attempts precisely this, and they all do so from a fundamentally interdisciplinary perspective. Social change is no respecter of the boundaries of disciplines and the tidy boxes that social scientists have often tried to squeeze it into. Above all, *Understanding Social Change* seeks to maintain and extend the Open University's democratic educational mission: to reach and enthuse an enormously diverse student population; to insist that critical, informed, reflexive engagement with the direction of social change is not a matter for elites and professional social scientists alone.

As you may have guessed, this series of books forms a core component of the Open University, Faculty of Social Sciences, level 1 course, DD100 *An Introduction to the Social Sciences: Understanding Social Change*. Each book in the series can be read independently of the other books and independently from the rest of the materials that make up the Open University course. However, if you wish to use the series as a whole, there are a number of references to chapters in other books in the series, and these are easily identifiable because they are printed in bold type.

Making the course and these books has been a long and complex process, and thanks are due to an enormous number of people.

First and foremost, the entire project has been managed and kept on the rails, when it was in mortal danger of flying off them, by our excellent Course Manager, Christina Janoszka. In the DD100 office, Fran Ford, Lesley Moore and Sylvia Lay-Flurrie have been the calm eye at the centre of a turbulent storm, our thanks to all of them. For the second edition we have had the much valued support of Matt Staples and Lydia Chant.

Stephen Clift, Chris Wooldridge and Penny Bennett have been meticulous, hawk-eyed editors. Siân Lewis has provided superb design work, and Ray Munns and Andy Whitehead have provided skilled cartographic and artistic work. David Calderwood and then Richard Golden in project control have arranged and guided the schedule with calm efficiency and Celia Hart has provided great support with illustrations and photographs. Nigel Thrift, our external assessor, and Clive Pearson, Elizabeth Chaplin and Lynne Poole, our tutor panel, provided consistent and focused criticism, support and advice. Peggotty Graham has been an invaluable friend of *Understanding Social Change* and David Held provided balance, perspective and insight as only he can.

It only remains for us to say that we hope you find *Understanding Social Change* an engaging and illuminating introduction to the social sciences, and in turn you find the social sciences essential for understanding life in the twenty-first century.

David Goldblatt
Kath Woodward
Co-Chairs, The Open University Course Team

Introduction

Kath Woodward

> We live in a world where identity matters. It matters both as a concept, theoretically, and as a contested fact of contemporary political life.
>
> (Gilroy, 1997, p.301)

Why is identity of interest to social scientists? Why does it matter now? The discussion of identity in this book is organized around three central questions, although each of these questions provokes further lines of enquiry. The first question is: *how are identities formed?* Identities are formed through interaction between people. When people take up different identities there are different processes taking place as people position themselves, and are positioned, in the social world. These processes include a focus on the personal dimensions of the identity equation as well as an interrogation of how these connect to the society in which we live. Casting a spotlight on the social aspects of identity leads us to explore the structures through which our lives are organized. Our identities are shaped by social structures but we also participate in forming our own identities. Which are the more important of these structures? We suggest that gender, class and culture (using the example of nation) are particularly important. These are introduced in Chapter 1 and become respectively the focus of Chapters 2, 3 and 4. We explore some of the processes involved when people interact with each other and the world around them.

Discussion of the role of social factors in identity formation raises the second framing question: *to what extent can we shape our own identities?* The changes which are identified are largely structural: in the economy, in new technologies, through migration and ethnic diversity, in the organization of domestic and family life, and in gender roles. How far do these structures constrain people and shape their identities and to what extent are people able to reconstruct themselves and their own identities? How can people influence social structures and use them to recreate collective identities? Identity necessarily involves an interrelationship between the personal and the social which can also be expressed as a tension between structure and agency. This tension is a key concern of the book.

The third framing question is: *are there particular uncertainties about identity at this moment in the UK?* There have been significant changes in forms of domestic living, family life and employment in the post-war period. Recent years have seen a proliferation of new technologies and communication systems which might appear to open up the possibility of transforming our daily lives. Such changes take place at the global level but have an impact on the UK. The structure of the UK is changing politically with devolution, separate assemblies and more explicit recognition of the political identities of

Wales, Scotland and Northern Ireland. The UK is a multicultural society with a diverse ethnic population which challenges the notion that being British means being white. Identities are changing and fluid and this very fluidity creates uncertainty and diversity, but what forms does the expression of uncertainty take? What possibilities are there for reconstruction through the formation of new identities? How do we seek to stabilize identities at a time of change and disruption?

Each of the three framing questions is about finding out and about producing knowledge, upon which it is possible to make claims about identity. This involves an introduction to some of the methods adopted by social scientists, as well as some discussion of the production of knowledge through culture – for example, through symbols such as language and visual images. Throughout the book we extend a social science critique which starts with questions which lead to claims, building up arguments by citing evidence which is then evaluated. Each chapter revisits the claims made in previous chapters and reconsiders the need for more evidence and different questions. The book as a whole thus develops cumulatively, with each chapter exploring different claims and seeking more evidence and developing explanations about how identities are formed.

In Chapter 1, 'Questions of Identity', Kath Woodward sets the scene by introducing the three central questions of the book. This chapter focuses on definitions of identity and on what social science can tell us about the ways in which identities are formed and how individuals make sense of themselves in the social world in which they live. The chapter highlights some of the key dimensions of identity: the social structures which might shape our sense of who we are – gender, class and nation. They are often the site of contradictory and competing identities, but each offers the possibility of some grounding for our understanding of ourselves and opportunities for diversity through forging new identities in changing times. Different social science approaches give more or less emphasis to the agency which can be exercised in taking up identities, but all involve some interrelationship between the personal and the social. This chapter introduces some of the ways in which knowledge about identities is produced, through first-person evidence, visual images and representations, as well as through social science critiques which draw upon such evidence.

In Chapter 2, 'Identity and Gender', Jennifer Gove and Stuart Watt focus on gender as a key source of identity. Gender might be seen to offer some grounding for identity. Does it? Where might we look to find out if being female or male might offer some basis for understanding the identities which people have? The first part of the chapter looks at what gender categories mean and how gender identities are formed in childhood. What sort of criteria do we use to classify people as women or as men and to distinguish between feminine and masculine behaviour? The chapter's focus on gendered performance in education offers a useful illustration both of change in a particular historical period (post-war to the present) and of apparent certainties, specifically boys' overachievement, being subverted and challenged by girls' recent success, for example, in public exams. This recent phenomenon, more complex than it at first appears, suggests both uncertainty and new opportunities and the possibility of restructuring gender stereotypes and forging new gender identities. Jennifer Gove and Stuart Watt consider the tensions between individual agency and social structures, especially the constraints of gender stereotypes and categories, in the shaping of gender identities. The chapter explores claims about gender categorization and looks at different sources of evidence, including empirical data, and at different theoretical explanations of gender difference.

In Chapter 3, 'Identity, Inequality and Social Class', Maureen Mackintosh and Gerry Mooney shift the focus on to the economic bases of identity and extend earlier discussion of difference to concentrate on inequality. At a time of change in patterns of employment in the UK, work-based identities are changing and may offer more uncertainty, as does the challenge to social class as a major determinant of who we are. However, economic factors, in particular poverty, must surely offer a bottom line in determining who we are. Or is the picture here more complex? The chapter explores some different social science explanations of class, drawing on the work of Karl Marx and Max Weber, and goes on to consider ways in which individuals and groups might actively engage in shaping their own identities. This introduces more recent debates about the relationship between production and consumption and the importance of lifestyle, where people, through the practice of consumption, can be seen as consuming identities.

In Chapter 4, '"Race", "Ethnicity" and Identity', Gail Lewis and Ann Phoenix move the spotlight again to address other dimensions of identity that have important historical resonance which is reflected in changes in the contemporary UK. How do race and ethnicity impact upon the formation of identities and what sort of processes are involved in the shaping of identities in the multi-ethnic UK? This chapter uses the questions posed in Chapter 1 to explore the relevance of race and ethnicity, for example in how we see ourselves and how we are seen by others, including official categories of ethnicity such as those used in the census. Is there more uncertainty about being British at this time? Are there more opportunities for shaping new identities through ethnic diversity? How can changes be effected and what is the role of collective agency in these processes? The chapter questions the idea that such identities, including whiteness, are fixed and discusses the parts played by race and ethnicity in the changes that are taking place in the UK.

The book is question led, as can be seen from the title! This is in keeping with the development of the critical approach to social science. Our approach is genuinely interdisciplinary. Those of us writing in this book come from the disciplines of sociology, psychology, economics and social policy and draw on the analyses of our own disciplines as well as recent interdisciplinary critiques of identity.

Reference

Gilroy, P. (1997) 'Diaspora and the detours of identity' in Woodward, K. (ed.) *Identity and Difference*, London, Sage/The Open University.

Questions of identity

Kath Woodward

Contents

1   QUESTIONS OF IDENTITY

This chapter is about questions of identity. Identity itself seems to be about a question, 'who am I?' We are going to focus on three key questions:

- How are identities formed?
- How much control do we have in shaping our own identities?
- Are there particular uncertainties about identity in the contemporary UK?

First, we need to think a bit more about what we mean by identity.

1.1   What is identity?

If identity provides us with the means of answering the question 'who am I?' it might appear to be about personality; the sort of person I am. That is only part of the story. Identity is different from personality in important respects. We may share personality traits with other people, but sharing an identity suggests some *active* engagement on our part. We choose to *identify* with a particular identity or group. Sometimes we have more choice than others. This chapter will address the relative importance of *structures*, the forces beyond our control which shape our identities, and *agency*, the degree of control which we ourselves can exert over who we are. Identity requires some awareness on our part. Personality describes qualities individuals may have, such as being outgoing or shy, internal characteristics, but identity requires some element of choice. For example, I may go to football matches on Saturdays because I enjoy shouting loudly with a crowd of lively extroverts, but I go to watch Sheffield Wednesday because I want to *identify* with that particular team, to wear that scarf and make a statement about who I am, and, of course, because I want to state that I support *one* Sheffield team and *not* the other (Sheffield United). We may be characterized by having personality traits, but we have to identify with – that is, actively take up – an identity.

This example also illustrates the importance of marking oneself as having the *same* identity as one group of people and a *different* one from others. Think about a situation where you meet someone for the first time and, in trying to find out who they are, ask questions about where they come from and what they do. In such situations we are trying to find out what makes up this person and also what makes them the *same* as us – that is, what we have in common – and what makes them *different*. If you see somebody wearing the badge of an organization to which you also belong, it marks that person out as being the same as you, as sharing an identity. Or consider a situation where, travelling abroad, hearing the voices of those who speak your own language, you feel both a sense of recognition and of belonging. In a strange place, finding people who share our language provides us with something and someone with whom we can identify. Or imagine that you are on a train, and a stranger in the compartment is reading the local newspaper from the town where you were born. You might strike up a conversation which includes references to what you have in common. This presents a moment of recognition and of having something in common with another person who shares an identity with you. Identity is marked by similarity, that is of the people like us, and by difference, of those who are not. There are other examples which are less reassuring, where the appropriate identity is *not* established, and where, for example, one may be denied access to credit or hire purchase, pension or sickness benefits, or entry to a club or restaurant, or, even more significantly, to a country.

How do we know which people are the same as us? What information do we use to categorize others and ourselves? In the examples above, what is often important is a *symbol*, like a badge, a team scarf, a newspaper, the language we speak, or perhaps the clothes we wear. Sometimes it is obvious. A badge can be a clear public statement that we identify with a particular group. Sometimes it is more subtle, but symbols and representations are important in marking the ways in which we share identities with some people and distinguish ourselves as different from others.

In this sense, although as individuals we have to take up identities actively, those identities are necessarily the product of the society in which we live and our relationship with others. Identity provides a link between individuals and the world in which they live. Identity combines how I see myself and how others see me. Identity involves the internal and the subjective, and the external. It is a socially recognized position, recognized by others, not just by me.

However, how I see myself and how others see me do not always fit. For example, individuals may view themselves as high achievers, worthy of promotion, yet be viewed by their employer as less than successful. The young people noisily returning home from a club in the early hours of the morning may be seen by others as troublemakers. Think about some of the ways in which how you see yourself may be at variance with others' perception of you. This could be at a more personal level, in the context of family and friendship relationships, or at a more public or even global level, where particular characteristics are attributed to specific national or ethnic groups. A sense of conflicting identities may result from the tensions between having to be a student, a parent, and an employee at the same time: these are examples of the *multiple identities* which people have.

The link between myself and others is not only indicated by the connection between how I see myself and how other people see me, but also by the connection between what I want to be and the influences, pressures and opportunities which are available. Material, social and physical constraints prevent us from successfully presenting ourselves in some identity positions – constraints which include the perceptions of others. Criminal identities are often produced through the exaggeration of stereotyping, where newspaper reports reproduce the notion of a criminal identity as young, male and black (Mooney *et al.*, 2000). Criminality can be produced by others who construct this category of person. This process of stereotyping certain groups as criminal also illustrates some of the imbalances and inequalities in the relationship between the individual and the world outside.

The subject, 'I' or 'we' in the identity equation, involves some element of choice, however limited. The concept of identity encompasses some notion of human agency; an idea that we can have some control in constructing our own identities. There are, of course, constraints which may lie in the external world, where material and social factors may limit the degree of agency which individuals may have. Lack of material resources severely limits the opportunities we have, as we will consider in the case of poverty and economic constraints in Chapter 3. It is impossible to have an identity as a successful career woman if one is without a job and if there are no employment opportunities. Other limitations to our autonomy may reside within us, for example in the bodies which we inhabit, as illustrated by the ageing process, by physical impairments, illness and the actual size and shape of our bodies.

SUMMARY

Identity involves:

- a link between the personal and the social;

- some active engagement by those who take up identities;

- being the same as some people and different from others, as indicated by symbols and representations;

- a tension between how much control I have in constructing my identities and how much control or constraint is exercised over me.

structure & agency

2   WHO AM I?

Let us start with an example of an individual and his identity which illustrates the link between the personal and the social. The social scientist Madan Sarup uses the example of his passport, which gives information about his identity in an official sense. Our passports name, describe and place us. A passport describes an individual; it names *one* person. It also states to which *group*, in particular which nation, that person belongs:

> I have three passports, all British ... In the first one, I am a young man with a lot of hair and a confident smile. My height is 5ft 8in and I am a school teacher. In my second passport photograph, most of the hair has gone. I have a white beard and a serious expression. My height is now 1.73 metres and I am a college lecturer. In the

third passport, the smaller red one, I am bald. Again I have a serious expression, but now my face is heavily lined. A friend asks: which is the *real* you? Of course, people see me in many different ways ... I want to have a closer look at my red passport ... At the top are the words 'European community' ... The passport refers to my nationality — British Citizen.

(Sarup, 1996, p.xiv)

FIGURE I.I   Examples of UK passports

Three passports offer details about identities, which are different, yet each belongs to the same person. Physical appearance is important, but it changes over time. Sarup's friend asks, 'which is the real you?' This suggests that there is not only continuity in the name of the person who possesses the passports, but that there might be a fixed, true, 'real' identity which could be uncovered. The personal identity of the named person includes their experience and life story. Continuity is important to our understanding of who we are, but changes suggest that identities are not fixed and constant; they change too.

We have some information here about what Sarup looks like. At one level physical appearance is how we 'read' people when we meet them. The body is also an important component of personal identity. Sarup cites physical appearance as the principal example of what is revealed here, but there are many other aspects of the body which have an impact on identity. Size, shape, disability, sex, all influence our experience of who we are and who we can be.

A passport picks out other key aspects of identity, which include occupation, nationality and age, all of which position us and give us a place in the society in which we live. However, it does not say anything about *how* we occupy these positions or about what they mean to us. We do not know how Sarup himself feels. Passport details cannot reveal a person's feelings. We need more information:

I think of [British Citizenship] as a formal category, because it does not express how I feel about it. I am not proud to be 'British'; it reminds me of the scars of imperialism, the days of the Raj. I feel more sympathetic to being a citizen of the

European Community, but here too I feel ambivalent. I would rather be a citizen of a federal European Community, but friends remind me that the concept of the 'Fortress Europe' is a Euro-centric strategy to maintain the power and privilege of the 'First World'.

(Sarup, 1996, p.xv)

Here Sarup suggests that he identifies more actively with being a European than a British citizen. To identify with a nation or group like this is to take up a *collective identity*. However, only one UK identity is offered by the passport. I notice that my own passport gives my place of birth, in Wales, but currently calls me a British and not a Welsh citizen. That Britain is a multi-ethnic, multicultural society is not acknowledged here either. Sarup refers to the colonial past which positions him in a particular relationship with 'Britishness'. This history is not recognized in the passport. The British Empire, however, used to have a place, with the old blue passport which referred to 'The United Kingdom of Great Britain and her Colonies', but the more recent EC and the new EU passports have no place for multi-ethnicity as yet. Those who hold the UK passport are grouped together as if we share one British identity. What we have in common is that we do not have another national identity (unless we have dual citizenship). We are not French or Chinese nationals. Identity is thus also marked by difference; that is, by indicating what we are not. We shall return to the importance of nation in the creation of identities in Chapter 4.

The very fact of having a passport at all confers identity. Particular passports provide rights of citizenship which are denied those who do not possess a passport at all. The passport illustrates some of the ways in which identities are institutionally constructed, and in this case the UK state, through legislation, plays a very powerful part in defining the identities of its citizens, especially in making some identities possible and others impossible. In the UK, birth has to be registered in order for the child to exist officially at all. Birth certificates, like death certificates, require that the person be classified as female or male. There is no alternative or scope for negotiation. At present, whatever an individual does in life to change their gender identity, the death certificate has to accord with the birth certificate, which cannot be changed retrospectively. Other examples of the official production and classification of an identity include ID cards, credit cards, membership cards, driving licences or any other sort of licence.

ACTIVITY 1.1

Think about your own passport or any other identity card or official document. What does it say about you? Does it suggest groups with whom you share an identity and those from whom you are different? Does this suggest several different identities? What is omitted? What is the importance of such institutional identities?

COMMENT

The kind of information revealed in an official document like a passport has many omissions about what identities and allegiances may be important in our daily lives. Fortunately, the state does not expose our political allegiances, community involvement, sexuality or status as a parent, although these also combine to produce our identities. The apparently single identity of citizenship leaves out all the contradictions about who we are and the multiplicity of identities each of us has.

Institutions like the state do have the power to restrict individual or collective freedom to adopt some identities. We probably do not think about these restrictions nor about national identity or citizenship very often, except when we are denied the rights associated with citizenship.

SUMMARY

- The passport example illustrates the tension between how I see myself and how I am seen by others, between the personal and the social.
- Institutions such as the state play an important role in constructing identities.
- Difference is very clearly marked in relation to national identity.
- Such official categories contain omissions and cannot fully accommodate the personal investment we have in our identities, nor the multiple identities we have.

In the next section we explore some of the ways in which social science can clarify some of the definitions of identity which have been offered and begin to address some of the questions which have been asked.

3   WHO ARE YOU? WHAT CAN SOCIAL SCIENCE TELL US?

In Sections 1 and 2, I argued that identity possessed the following characteristics:

- It links how I see myself and how others see me.
- It links the individual and the social.
- It is marked by similarity and difference.
- It involves some active engagement on our part and a tension between human agency and social structures.

- There are single and multiple identities.
- Identities can be seen as fixed or fluid and changing.

In this section we return to the definition of identity and ask how social scientists have attempted to address these two questions:

How are identities formed?

How much control do we have in the construction of our identities?

3.1   Imagining ourselves

The work of the social philosopher George Herbert Mead, published in the 1930s, has been extensively used in thinking about identity because he offered useful insights into the link between how we see ourselves and the ability of human beings to *imagine* how others might see us (Mead, 1934). Mead focuses on the processes that are involved in linking the internal and the external. Think about it this way. Imagine that you have an interview for a job. You think about the interview before the 'big day' and consider what to wear. You want to look smart but perhaps that new suit would be too hot and you would end up feeling, and looking, very uncomfortable, especially if the heating was turned up high. Maybe you should try not to look too formal? What is going on here? In order to make the decision about what to wear you have to imagine yourself, to look at yourself from the outside. We have to think about how others see us and to be self-conscious. Mead argued that it is the capacity to imagine how others would see us and our capacity to carry images in our heads which is an important distinguishing feature of human beings. For Mead, identities are produced in a social context, but through individuals thinking about what links them to the social world. We do this, he argued, through **symbolizing**. This is best illustrated in our use of language, where words operate as symbols. Pictures, images and gestures are also symbolic in that they too *represent* something else. A symbol stands for something else. For example, the word 'table' stands for the object which we call a table. Having the word allows us to talk and think about the object, namely the table, even when there is no table within view. The suit worn at the interview in the scenario above signifies or stands for the serious candidate. We symbolize the sort of person we want others to think we are through the clothes we wear and the ways in which we behave. In the interview example we have an image of ourselves at the interview, either in the disastrous overheated scenario or preferably in another more confident, successful scene where we might *visualize* ourselves appropriately dressed and getting the job.

Symbolizing
Making one object, word or image stand for or signify another. For example, a red light at traffic lights symbolizes 'stop', and green means 'you can go'.

Symbols and representations are important in the production of identities. This is how we signal our identities to others and how we know which people we identify with and those who are distinguished as being different. How we speak, the clothes we wear, badges, scarves, uniforms or flags all offer symbols of identity. Judith Williamson, whose work focuses on representational systems, writing within the discipline of cultural studies, describes the process of choosing an identity in the following way:

> When I rummage through my wardrobe in the morning I am not merely faced with the choice of what to wear. I am faced with the choice of images: the difference between a smart suit and a pair of overalls, a leather skirt and a cotton skirt, is not one of fabric and style, but one of identity. You know perfectly well that you will be seen differently for the whole day, depending on what you put on; you will appear as a particular kind of woman with one particular identity which excludes others. The black leather skirt rather rules out girlish innocence, oily overalls tend to exclude sophistication ... often I have wished I could put them all on together – just to say, 'how dare you think any of these is me. But also, see, I can be all of them'.
>
> (Williamson, 1986, p.91)

Williamson suggests that we can choose the image that we present to others. She assumes that we have a choice, and that we know other people will understand our choices. In different cultures, these clothes, for example, would be interpreted in very different ways.

How does this develop our understanding of identity? Considering the claim that identity involves how I see myself and how others see me has led to some suggestions about how this takes place. First, we have to be able to imagine ourselves, to reflect on who we are and how we appear to others. Second, we do this through symbolizing, through producing images and visualizing ourselves. The ability to visualize ourselves and to represent ourselves gives us some degree of agency, although the repetoire of symbols upon which we can draw is always limited by the particular culture which we inhabit, as illustrated in the quotation from Williamson. This approach to the notion of identity puts more emphasis on the control which individuals have, rather than the constraints which they experience.

SUMMARY

- In constructing identities we imagine ourselves.
- We do this by visualizing ourselves, thinking in symbols.
- Who I am is dependent on how I am seen by others as well as how I see myself.

In addressing the question about how identities are formed we have focused on the processes which are involved in constructing an identity within the individual; what happens in the social situation is left out. What else do we need to know? What happens when people present themselves to others, in everyday interaction?

3.2 Everyday interaction

Erving Goffman, the sociologist whose work has been very influential in sociology and social psychology, focused on analysis of everyday interaction, conversations and encounters. How do we communicate with others? Goffman suggested that how we present ourselves to others was rather like acting out a part in a play where the scripts are already written. In the work which we discuss here he refers to roles not to identities, but his focus on the detail of everyday interaction is also useful in exploring how we understand the identities of others and how we present ourselves. He based his work on a theatrical metaphor. He states in his book *The Presentation of Self in Everyday Life* (1959) that his perspective on the self is dramaturgical – that is, based on the idea of a performance. What we are is not given (that is, there already), it must be created. We act out in a whole range of different **roles** which are rather like parts in a play. Actors in a play cannot act out any old part and say what they like. They have to speak the lines written. However, even if the roles are written we can improvise and interpret our roles, although there are constraints.

Individuals, like actors, are performing for an audience. Speech, acts and gestures all require someone else to be watching or listening. The parts we play may be already written but we bring our own expectations and interpretations to these roles. We have to be convincing in order to persuade others in the audience that this is an authentic part that we are playing. For example, as a student you have to persuade your tutor that this is a serious role – that you are *really* a student. How do you do this? Perhaps you ensure that you submit your assignments on time, look earnest, carry piles of books around with you and deny any involvement in late-night party-going? The bank manager, the teacher or the doctor; each has to give a performance which convinces others of their authenticity. This is not quite the same as investing in an identity – that is, having personal commitment to an identity – but it does give us more detail about how we 'read' people and about how we get the message about 'who they are'.

> **Roles**
> The society into which we are born presents us with a series of roles, which are patterns of behaviour, routines and responses, like parts in a play.

A society like the contemporary UK offers a whole range of social roles which we as individuals can take up. Stop and think for a moment about the number of such positions that you occupy – in your home life, in familial relationships, at work, as a consumer, as a citizen, as a client of the welfare state or social or medical services. This involves a combination of our own expectations about a role and those of the society in which we live.

Not all of our actions in these scenarios are conscious or explicit. Sometimes we give information to other people directly. In these instances Goffman describes the public display which we intend to make when we *give* information as front stage. Appearance, clothes and gestures are crucial in the presentation of self, but sometimes the information presented may inadvertently reveal more about a person than the information directly or intentionally given. We *give off* information which we do not quite intend; for example, the nervous interview candidate who twists his fingers unintentionally is *giving off* an impression of anxiety whilst attempting to give a confident performance. The friend who is trying to look interested but who is all the while drumming her fingers and looking around may be *giving off* an impression of boredom.

The focus of Goffman's work is on everyday interactions. It offers us more ideas about answers to our first question at the beginning of Section 3: how are identities formed? His emphasis is on the social dimensions of identity and the relationship between identity, with its concern with personal investment, and roles which tells us more about the social aspects and social exchanges between people. Goffman's approach suggests that there are links between the society in which we live and the limitations offered by the roles or parts we play in that society, because the scripts have, in a sense, already been written. However, there is also scope for agency because those who play the parts can improvise and offer their own interpretation.

There are some important features of Goffman's original theory which contribute to our understanding of identity and which offer more detail about how identities are presented in linking the personal and the social:

- All performances are addressed to an audience.
- Information can be given intentionally or *given off*, where we might reveal things unintentionally.

What is the source of the information which is *given off*, revealed without our consciously intending to do so? Identity relies upon a conscious, active presentation, but it might also involve thoughts and feelings about which we might not be conscious. Unintentional signs, 'slips of the tongue' are manifestations of the *unconscious* mind.

3.3 The unconscious

What mechanisms, of which we might not be consciously aware, determine our identities? Sigmund Freud's psychoanalytic theory gives us some ways in which to answer this question. One of the major contributions of Freudian psychoanalysis is his understanding of the **unconscious**, an idea which has passed into everyday language in Western societies through popular culture, the advertising industry and through psychoanalytically inspired practices like therapy. Think about the language in problem pages or used on television in the personal confession programmes on daytime TV.

Unconscious
The unconscious mind is the repository of repressed feelings and desires – often from childhood. These feelings can emerge, for example, in dreams. They can influence the choices we make in later life.

STANLEY WAS DEEPLY DISAPPOINTED WHEN, HIGH IN THE TIBETAN MOUNTAINS, HE FINALLY FOUND HIS TRUE SELF.

You may be familiar with the idea of *Freudian slips,* when the word we actually say is not the word we intended, which reveals something about our hidden desires. There may be occasions on which you have said one thing when you meant another and what you have said has been embarrassing or humorous. I can think of an example in a handwritten essay where the student wrote 'of coffee' instead of 'of course', suggesting that it might have been time for a break! Another wrote 'sexy' instead of 'sexist' in an essay on gender, which might indicate other preoccupations in the unconscious mind rather than feminist critiques of social institutions. Freud argued that these slips along with jokes and dreams can reveal our 'true' feelings.

The unconscious is separate from the conscious mind and has its own rules and its own language. Freud argued, based on case studies of people he had analysed, that through early development children repress all their anti-social needs and wants, all the things a child is not allowed to do or to have. This repressed material enters the unconscious and, although it cannot be directly accessed by the conscious mind, is revealed in dreams or slips of the tongue (see Bocock, 1983). Who we are is not given in advance, we are not born with an identity, but it emerges in a number of different forms through a series of identifications which combine and emerge in an infinite number of forms so there is never one fixed, coherent identity but several in play.

You will recall that in the definition of identity in Section 1.1 it was suggested that we have to identify with an identity – that is, actively engage with a position. It is not enough to be classified by someone else, we have to take it up ourselves; for example, identify with a political party or a social movement or with enthusiasts for a type of music. **Identification** is a term often associated with psychoanalysis. Identification does not just involve copying; it involves taking that identity *into* yourself. Freud focused on male children and suggests that the little boy is especially interested in his father, although he loves his mother. He wants to grow up like his father and to take his place.

Psychoanalysis is one of the social theories which is organized around a concern with sex, sexuality and gender. In Freud's approach, children are seen as having sexual desires of a diverse kind. Some of these desires are repressed into the unconscious. Freud argued that the most important psychological drive is sexuality. By sexuality he meant a broad category of pleasure-seeking desires which are experienced even by newborn babies, who, for example, derive pleasure from sucking. If a child's needs are met in

Identification
The psychological process of association between oneself and something else (originally someone else).

infancy, the child is more likely to develop into an adult with a positive outlook on life, whereas the child whose needs are not met will grow up with a pessimistic, negative disposition.

Not only did Freud argue that children were sexual but also that the most significant aspect of development was psycho-sexual. Identification with the parent of the same sex was vital for the satisfactory development of the child into adulthood. This has implications for our exploration of identity. Freud's focus on the unconscious adds to our understanding of the processes at work in the formation of identities. It suggests that we bring childhood experiences, even those about which we are not conscious, to the decisions we make as adults. This might suggest that we have limited control over the identities which we take up. They may be determined by this early childhood experience. However, Freud argues that we may be able to exercise more agency through coming to an understanding of those things which we have repressed into our unconscious minds from childhood experience, notably through therapy which can help us to understand ourselves.

The importance of psychoanalytic theory for our investigation of identity can be summarized as follows:

- The identity positions which we take up may be the result of unconscious feelings which we may try to rationalize but which we do not know for sure.

- Many aspects of identity derive from childhood experience so that identity is constructed by the past as well as through the present.

- Identity is not fixed and unchanging, but the result of a series of conflicts and of different identifications.

- Both gender and sexuality are important to our understanding of identity. Our sense of who we are is most significantly linked to our awareness of our identities as women or as men.

Structure and agency in Section 3

Section 3 has focused on the question of how identities are formed and some of the processes which are involved when people take up identities and present these to other people. As we have seen, identity presents a link between the personal – that is, individuals taking up identities – and the social – that is, the social situations in which people find themselves, including social roles, everyday interactions with others and the language which we use. These accounts of identity formation offer different emphases on the role of individuals in shaping their own identities. How do these accounts address our second question?

How much control do we have in shaping our own identities?

Table 1.1 illustrates how each of the approaches discussed in Section 3 addresses this question. Each involves an interrelationship between agency and structure, but some offer more scope for agency.

TABLE 1.1

	Agency	Structure
Mead	Visualization, symbolization, imagination of individuals. We have autonomy in imagining ourselves	We have to use existing language and symbols
Goffman	Negotiation of roles; we can interpret the parts we play	The parts or scripts have already been written for the roles we play
Freud	Individuals can come to understand their childhood experience and shape their own identities. Identities are never completely fixed	Social forces can operate through the unconscious, which shapes our identities

4 LINKING THE PERSONAL AND THE SOCIAL

Identity presents the interface between the personal – what is going on inside our heads, how we as individuals feel about who we are – and the social – the societies in which we live and the social, cultural and economic factors which shape experience and make it possible for people to take up some identities and render others inaccessible or impossible. In this section, we look at other views of how identities are formed, continuing to address our first question, but shifting the emphasis on to the social aspect of the identity equation, so that we can begin to consider the third question about uncertainty and about how identities change. In order to explore the possibility that there might be some uncertainties about who we are in the contemporary UK, we need to look in more detail at the relationship between changing social structures and changing identities.

4.1 Hey you! Who me? Interpellation

What happens when individuals take up a particular identity position? You will recall that in the earlier discussion in Section 3.1 we considered the importance of symbolization and the ways in which human beings can imagine themselves occupying a particular identity. What is actually happening when we imagine ourselves as the successful candidate, the streetwise teenager or the sporting hero? Why do some identities 'work' so that we are drawn into them?

One important attempt to resolve the problem of where the individual stands in relation to socially constructed and even determined identity positions was developed by Louis Althusser who argued that when people are recruited into identity positions they are **interpellated** or hailed (Althusser, 1971).

It works like this. Imagine that you are walking down the street and someone calls out your name. You stop, turn round and think 'that's me, they're calling me'. Althusser argued that this is how we come to feel that an identity is the one which fits us – as a member of a religious community, as a New Labour voter, as a lad, as a mother, as a 'new man', as a European. The process is one of recognition, of looking at yourself and thinking 'that's me'! Advertising offers plenty of opportunities to think about how this works. Let me show

Interpellation
A process whereby people recognize themselves in a particular identity and think 'that's me'.

FIGURE I.2 Domestic bliss: the appeal of home life (when 'gay' had a different meaning)

FIGURE 1.3   Women in the workplace: the independent mother

you an example of how some women, as mothers, might have felt 'yes that's me' in the 1950s and more recently. In the 1950s, women's magazines encouraged women, who might have worked outside the home during the wartime, to return to their domestic duties. Women were actively recruited into being housewives and mothers. Some might have felt that was the sort of mother they wanted to be, and that they fitted this identity. Women's magazines at this time sought to both promote this notion of motherhood and to enable their readers to identify with it (see Figure 1.2).

Such promotions were used in the 1950s to encourage women back into the home and into domesticity. This example illustrates a maternal identity at a particular moment in history. By the late 1990s a rather different maternal identity was being presented and, if the figures for women's participation in the labour market and the sale of women's magazines are to be believed, this is an identity which had purchase at this time (see Figure 1.3). By 1999, mothers might have been more likely to be 'hailed' by the pregnant woman in the workplace than by images of domestic bliss. Advertisements in women's magazines at this time plug into mothers' concerns with juggling paid work and child care.

Advertisements present us with commodities which are promoted as part of a lifestyle. Consumers can purchase symbols of the identities that they want to possess.

Can you think of examples of such advertisements which seek to interpellate the consumer in particular ways? Those for cars, for example? What sort of associations are you expected to make? Would buying a particular model of car make you seem successful, sexy, modern?

Next time you see advertisements on television or in newspapers or magazines, think about the identities which you are being invited to adopt by association.

SUMMARY

- Interpellation links the individual to the social.
- It may work consciously or unconsciously.

The work of social scientists which has been considered so far has given us more information about the processes whereby identities are formed. Some of the views discussed focused on the individual and on the details of social interaction rather than the broader picture of social structures which might constrain us. Althusser's work sought to link the individual and the social and to show how some social structures work to recruit people into identities. What can social science tell us about the ways in which these structural aspects of society shape our identities? What are these social structures? Are some more important than others? Are they changing?

4.2 Social structures: concepts and explanations

At this point, I am going to shift the emphasis from personal identity in the context of everyday situations to some of the social structures, such as occupation, nation, and gender, which I suggested in Section 2 were significant influences on identity. How do social scientists explain these structures? I picked out work, gender and nation, ethnicity and place as being useful examples. Each of the remaining chapters of this book focuses on one of these aspects of identity but they are introduced here to signpost what follows and to offer some preliminary discussion of the concepts which are used.

One of the ways in which social scientists have attempted to explain work-based identities is to relate them to class. Social **class** is used by social scientists as a means of classifying the economic and social divisions of a society. Different economic systems create social class groupings, which involve some degree of inequality. Chapter 3 offers a fuller discussion of different analyses of class, but it is included here as an important factor influencing the life chances and identities of those who share a class position. The *unequal* distribution of material resources is a key feature of class division.

Class
Class is a large grouping of people who share common economic interests, experiences and lifestyles.

Another source of inequality can be found in **gender** relations (gender and identity are discussed in more detail in Chapter 2). There are areas of the labour market and of domestic work, including unpaid caring work within the home, which are seen as 'men's work' or 'women's work'. In industrial societies, paid work is exchanged for remuneration and is hence more valued and has higher status than unpaid domestic work or caring work. The former has been seen as masculine and the latter as feminine. This has been enacted in most Western societies through the notion of a male breadwinner which is primary to a man's identity, whereas women's work has been seen as an extension of their roles as wives and mothers and thus as a secondary activity.

Gender
Gender describes the systematic structuring of certain behaviour and practices which are associated with women or with men in particular societies.

This indicates the importance of gender as part of the organization of a society and not just a part of each individual's experience. It is part of the

Culture

The culture of a society is its shared meanings, values and practices. Culture provides us with some of the categories and means of organizing ideas through which we make sense of our lives.

culture of a society. Assumptions about what is appropriate for women and for men can shape and influence our identities and the scope which we have for deciding both 'who we are' and 'who we want to be'.

National identity is an important part of the culture of a society. Think back to the example of the passport, in Section 2. It highlighted the importance of place, of where we come from and of institutional constructions of citizenship. The passport was proof of British citizenship but obscured gender and ethnic differences. Rights of citizenship can provide people with either considerable freedom or with restraint. Not only were women not accorded the same voting rights as men in the UK until 1928, but other rights, for example to welfare benefits, have depended on gender. The rights conferred by citizenship are often gender-related. In the UK, rights to civil citizenship have depended on gender because historically the main criterion for citizenship has been independence, based mainly on economic status. Carole Pateman argues that:

> men, but not women, have been seen as possessing the capacities required of 'individuals', 'workers' and citizens' through the dichotomy breadwinner/housewife and the masculine meaning of independence. A 'worker' became a man who has an economically dependent wife to take care of his daily needs and look after his home and children ...
>
> (Pateman, 1992, p.228)

The purpose of this example about gendered citizenship here is to illustrate the importance of gender in the construction of identities like those of the worker and the citizen, and to stress the importance of these different interrelated aspects of social organization.

SUMMARY

- The organization of society is important in shaping our identities.
- Class, gender, ethnicity and place are important dimensions of identity.
- These factors illustrate the tension between the individual and the social and between the individual's control or agency and that of social structures.

In Section 3 we briefly examined some of the explanations and concepts which social science offers in response to the two questions posed at the start: How are identities formed? How much control can we exercise over the construction of our identities? The discussion in Section 4 focused on the relationship between individuals and social structures. Changing social structures – for example, changing gender roles, patterns of employment, changing class and ethnic composition of the UK – might mean different identities are becoming available and others are disappearing. What sort of social changes have taken place in the last 50 years? In the next section we look more carefully at the changing times.

5   WHO ARE WE?

Why are we interested in identity at this point in history? Identity is certainly something of interest to academics, as illustrated by the number of books and even whole courses organized around the subject, but why should this be the case at this moment in time? Could current concerns about identity be a reflection of broad social and cultural uncertainties produced by rapid social change?

Stop and think for a moment about some of the differences between your own life and that of your parents or grandparents. What social changes might these experiences represent? What are the differences, in terms of family, marriage, divorce, parenting, work – paid and unpaid?

One of the most significant changes in the post-war period has been the move away from heavy manufacturing industry, for example steel production, ship manufacturing and coal-mining, and the increase in service sector work. Evidence shows that in the 1950s only 21 per cent of married women were in paid employment (EOC, 1981). Now the vast majority of women, married and unmarried, are in paid work or seeking work, albeit often part-time work on short-term contracts (*Social Trends*, 2002).

Whereas in the 1950s and 1960s 90 per cent of people in the UK married at least once in their lives, in 2002 the figure was down to 70 per cent with nearly half of those who marry predicted to divorce. This is very different from the number of divorces prior to the 1969 Divorce Reform Act, when the proportion was 4 per cent. At the beginning of the twenty-first century more people married late if they did marry, at an average age of 29 rather than 21 as was the case in the 1950s. The number of births to never-married single mothers was the fastest growing family group in the UK in 2002.

Of course there are continuities; children have to be born and to be looked after, but how and by whom? What does it mean to be a mother or a father in the twenty-first century? Is it very different from the experience of our grandparents' generation? Should mothers or fathers stay at home to look after young children, should parents pay for child care or should the state or employers provide nurseries? Even those things which we might have thought to be immutable, rooted in biological certainty, have been challenged – for example, through the use of IVF (in-vitro fertilization), a reproductive technology which enabled Liz Buttle, a 60-year-old grandmother, to give birth in 1998. New technologies appear to challenge certainties and the constraints of biology, opening up questions about 'who we are' in situations where we might have thought there was no question. All of these social changes, economic, social and technological, present questions about identity. How do we construct ourselves, for example as parents or as workers, when society's expectations are changing and new technologies create new, hitherto unthought of, possibilities? The sociologist, Anthony Giddens, has argued (1991) that these questions are a feature of contemporary life in the West. Giddens maintains that identities become both more uncertain and more diverse in a rapidly changing globalized culture.

- Social changes taking place at global and personal levels can produce uncertainties in relation to who we are and our place in the world.
- Change is characterized by uncertainties and insecurities as well as by diversity and opportunities for the formation of new identities.

5.1 Is there a crisis?

Kobena Mercer, the cultural critic, argues that 'Identity only becomes an issue when it is in crisis' (Mercer, 1990). Is it 'in crisis?' There is evidence that this may be the case, for example in the ethnic and national conflicts across the world. Michael Ignatieff (1993) argues that one explanation of current concern with identity is that it is a useful explanatory concept providing a means of exploring conflict in the global context, such as in former Yugoslavia, in Rwanda, in parts of the former USSR and in Ireland. Identity matters. People have a strong personal investment in political and ethnic identities, even to the extent of being willing to die for them. In such contexts, crisis might be the appropriate word.

On which other occasions have you encountered the word 'crisis', for example in the news media? The term is also employed in media constructions of social change within the UK, for example in relation to familial relations such as the increase in divorce, lone parenting and teenage pregnancies which have been identified as a 'crisis in the family' and linked to the 'crisis in masculinity', manifest in boys' underachievement at school, which is discussed in Chapter 2, or in deviant behaviour by young men (Mooney *et al.*, 2004). Such examples may involve overstatement and a failure to address the complexities of the situations in which people find themselves. Uncertainty is not only characterized by crises. It also offers opportunities and greater diversity.

In the remainder of this chapter we are going to look at some examples of questions which involve situations where changes lead us to explore the issue of who we are and what we can now be. Uncertainty is not a new historical phenomenon but it is given different expression at different times. Have the goalposts been moved, or, perhaps more appropriately, are we now expected to play by different rules and wear a new strip?

SUMMARY

- Contemporary concerns with identity have been described as crises.
- There are also opportunities offered by the changes which are taking place.
- There are continuities as well as changes.

What are the particular uncertainties about identity at this point in history? A possible starting-point for finding out how uncertainties are expressed is to ask someone whose own life has changed.

6 WHAT DO YOU DO?

When we meet someone for the first time we are quite likely to ask them what they do in order to find out more about 'who they are'. A whole set of associated ideas about the person's identity may follow. The following extract is by John Greaves. John worked at the coal-face at Goldthorpe pit, South Yorkshire, for 20 years. For social scientists this is a particular form of evidence. It gives us information from a personal point of view. Here, in a piece of writing produced at a 'Return to Learn' course, run by the trade union UNISON and the Worker's Educational Association for unemployed miners, John describes the contrast between the mining village of Goldthorpe before 1984 and in 1997, 13 years after the pit was closed down.

ACTIVITY 1.2

Read the extract and think about these questions:

What does this autobiographical piece of writing tell us about identity?

How does John identify with the community and place in which he lived and worked?

How much control do you think John is able to exercise over the identities which he might want to adopt?

How important are social divisions like class and gender in the formation of those identities?

What are the uncertainties expressed here?

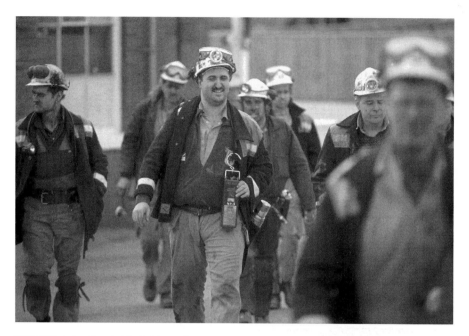

FIGURE 1.4   South Yorkshire miners

READING 1.1

John Greaves: 'The walk to work'

Pre-1984

Woken at 4 am by a twin belled wind up alarm clock, placed out of arms' reach. Boil the kettle while having a wash and brush up. Fill a flask, snatch a quick cup of tea before making off for the day shift at Goldthorpe Colliery. Flask in pocket, acme snap tin under my arm I make my way along Furlong Road, which is busy with similar looking men travelling to their work ... The odd pair of bicycles would creak past, no matter where you worked everyone said good morning or something of the like when passing. Passing the Jungle Club at five to five the odd light would still be burning, with a customer or two still putting the world to rights, or maybe they were piloting a round the clock drinking licence. Crossing the railway bridge on the sound of diesel locomotive pulling coal wagons away from the pit. Turning into Goldthorpe's Main Street just as the five o'clock buzzer at Hickleton Colliery was sounding. Three out of Goldthorpe's five butchers' shops would have been swept and swilled down, and the owners inside cutting and slicing ready for the day's trading. All three newsagents were brightly lit, with placards outside promising news hot off the press. By far most popular was Barry's, he had lost his right arm up to the shoulder as a young man. But an artist when it came to folding newspapers, or distributing chewing gum, snuff or cigarettes. All ... would soon be discussing Saturday's match, or who would win the 3.30 at Doncaster, while Barry struggled on manfully with his task. Once served, onward towards the Pit Lane with the mouth watering smell of fresh baked bread drifting from Mr Brown's Bakers shop past all the well kept shop fronts, then reaching the Goldthorpe Hotel, which was also taking part in the open all hours scheme. Into the Pit Lane, a long concrete road with a swing park, football pitches and rugby pitches on the left and, on the right an allotment site with a shanty town of huts and greenhouses, a few with smoking chimneys. The first stop in the pit yard was the time office ... Then making a move for the pit head baths, this was where the transformation took place from normal human being into a coal miner. Off with jeans and tee shirt and on with bright orange overalls, helmet, knee pads and steel toe capped boots. Fill a large plastic bottle with drinking water before going into the hot acid smelling area known as the lamp cabin. On with a cap lamp and battery and out the

FIGURE 1.5 The National Coal Board recruits for a job with a future (below). This advertisement appeared in a football programme, October 1961 (left)

other side for a breath of fresh air, before being searched for smoking materials. Boarding the paddy train along with another 120 men to be lowered down the tunnel known as the drift, to where we worked in the black water sodden seam, that was called by people locally 'The Sludge'. Everybody was happy, hard worked but happy.

The NCB recruiting posters used to say 'A Job for Life'.

1997

Woken by a noisy milk float at 4.10 am, boiled the kettle, made a cup of tea. No need for the flask these days, and the wash and brush up seems less important. Set off for a walk, into Furlong Road towards Goldthorpe, not a soul in sight, not a house light on. Then a sign of life, a postman whistles by on his regulation Royal Mail bicycle on his way to Goldthorpe small sorting office, again I am alone. Reaching the Jungle Club at five to five, paint flaking, all in darkness no more all night sitting, too many empty pockets. Crossing the railway bridge no longer the sound of locomotives pulling coal wagons. Looking over into the cutting is a depressing sight, rails that once shone now rusting, grass growing over the once well maintained sleepers and ballast. Landing on Goldthorpe's main street at five o'clock the buzzer does not sound anymore, Hickleton Colliery no longer exists. No butchers sweeping and swilling, only one newsagent open. 'Mick's News' has retired, the shop has been extended,

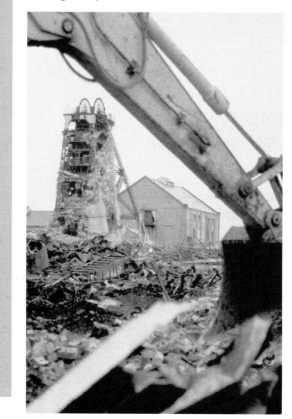

FIGURE 1.6 Demolition of a colliery, South Yorkshire

brightened but lacks customers. Walking towards the Pit Land passing boarded up shops that once thrived, no longer the smell of fresh baked bread. It seems the only new traders are second hand dealers. Reaching the Goldthorpe Hotel all in darkness, silent. Turning into the pit lane to find grass growing out of every crack and joint in the concrete road. What happened to the dozens of lorries and their drivers, that used to travel this way? The pavement that was once trodden by hundreds of men a day has been lost to the grass verge. Passing the swing park, seats broken the rocking horse on its side dead! Both the football and rugger pitches look in good condition, the council took them over. The shanty town on the allotment site is thriving, perhaps looked after by people in search of the 'good life'. Into the pit yard, no time office, no canteen, no pit head baths. Just odd bits of rubble left of what was the life blood of the local community. Going down to what was the mouth of the drift, all that's left there is a steel pipe coming up from the ground, to drain away gas from underground workings. It stands like a monument to all the men who worked there, and to some who lost their lives there.

The NCB recruiting poster used to say 'A Job for Life'.

Source: John Greaves

C O M M E N T

Although John does not use the word identity, his account focuses on his sense of who he is, especially as a member of a community located within a specific *place*. In the pre-1984 period, John made sense of himself by being part of a community with a *collective identity*. Pre-1984, John was interpellated by that collective identity. By 1997 he had lost that identification.

Post-1997, his identity is fragmented and uncertain. His account tells us that this personal sense of who we are is closely tied to having a shared position linked to work (in particular, to paid work), community and place. John has lost the identity of being part of a coal-mining community which has gone with the closure of the pits. He describes economic and material changes and his regret, not only for loss of financial security, but also for the loss of a sense of belonging and the symbols with which it was associated. There is nostalgia for past security and an ambivalence about the present. What is most striking about the reconstruction of the past is the importance of the material basis of identity and its links here with paid work.

Remember the question posed in Section 5, about the extent to which there might be greater uncertainty about identity at this historical moment. An area of life which seemed to offer certainty ('a job for life'), with a clearly defined identity and sense of belonging, no longer does so. This change in economic structure and in employment forces individuals to redefine themselves. It indicates that identities are not secure but fluid and that they are constantly being re-created and redefined. The concept of identity is used here to link how people feel inside and social and material changes around them. But the extract only gives us a feel for the situation from one person's perspective. We need more and different types of evidence. Chapter 3 will look at another kind of evidence, namely quantitative, statistical evidence, that describes some of these economic changes.

The dilemma presented in this first-person narrative tells us more about the process of identity formation and about which factors might be important. What are the important dimensions of identity here? Remember the aspects of social structure which we addressed in Section 4.2. The *unequal* distribution of material resources as a feature of class division illustrated in John Greaves's account highlights the impact of structural economic change, in the form of the closure of coal-mines, on individuals' life chances and perceptions of who they are. Whilst most social scientists accept that economic changes, especially since the Second World War, have affected class relations, the impact of class on identity is debated. Class is one factor which influences identity. In John's example, although class and work-based identity may seem particularly important, other social structures also impact on the individual's experience. Coal-mining was, and is, where it still exists in the UK, a predominantly male activity with a whole string of associations about the male breadwinner and a particular brand of masculinity linked to hard physical labour.

Thus, the personal narrative also indicated the links between *class* and *gender*, where uncertainty about employment and sources of income are paralleled by uncertainty about gendered identity, notably that of the male breadwinner. Significantly higher numbers of women are in paid employment in the first decade of the twenty-first century than in the 1950s, although women's pay is still only 75 per cent of men's (*Social Trends*, 2002). Although young women and men start out earning similar incomes, men's earnings exceed women's in mid life, when men's earnings are double those of women (*Social Trends*, 2002). All of these material changes have an impact on how women and men see themselves and offer structural constraints within which people have to negotiate their identities.

- A first-person narrative account offers one sort of evidence of the link between the personal and the social in the formation of identities.

- The work we do is an important factor influencing the identities which we can take up.

- This example indicates the influence of structural factors, including class and gender.

- The areas of experience addressed here suggest changing times and some degree of uncertainty about 'who we are?' in relation to 'what we are'.

In the next section we turn to another of the 'everyday' questions that we
might ask when we meet someone for the first time, after 'what do you do?':
Where do you come from?

7 WHERE DO YOU COME FROM? RACE AND PLACE

The following poem was written by Jackie Kay who was born in Glasgow in
1961. Her mother was a white Scottish woman and her father was a black
Nigerian student. She has written extensively about the subject of identity in
the context of her own experience – for example, of being an adopted child,
brought up in Glasgow.

ACTIVITY 1.3

Now read the poem.

SO YOU THINK I'M A MULE?

'Where do you come from?'
'I'm from Glasgow.'
'Glasgow?'
'Uh huh. Glasgow.'
The white face hesitates
the eyebrows raise
the mouth opens
then snaps shut
incredulous
yet too polite to say outright
liar
she tries another manoeuvre
'And you parents?'
'Glasgow and Fife.'
'Oh?'
'Yes. Oh?'
Snookered she wonders where she should go
from here –
'Ah, but you're not pure'
'Pure? Pure what.
'Pure white? Ugh. What a plight
Pure? Sure I'm pure
I'm rare ...'
'Well, that's not exactly what I mean,

I mean ... you're a mulatto, just look at ...'
'Listen. My original father was Nigerian
to help with your confusion
But hold on right there
If you Dare mutter mulatto
hover around hybrid
hobble on half-caste
and intellectualize on the
'mixed race problem'
I have to tell you:
take your beady eyes offa my skin;
don't concern yourself with
the 'dialectics of mixtures';
don't pull that strange blood crap
on me Great White Mother.
Say, I'm no mating of a
she-ass and a stallion
no half of this and half of that
to put it plainly purely
I am Black
My blood flows evenly, powerfully
and when they shout 'Nigger'
and you shout 'Shame'
ain't nobody debating my blackness.
You see that fine African nose of mine,
my lips, my hair, You see lady
I'm not mixed up about it.
So take your questions, your interest,
your patronage. Run along.
Just leave me.
I'm going to my Black sisters
to women who nourish each other
on belonging
There's a lot of us
Black women struggling to define
just who we are
where we belong
and if we know no home
we know one thing:
we are Black
we're at home with that.'
'Well, that's all very well, but ...'
'I know it's very well.
No But. Good bye.'

Source: Kay, 1991

What is meant by the question 'where do you come from?'?

What is the relationship being drawn between place and identity here?

What does Kay mean when she writes 'I am Black' and then 'we are Black'?

COMMENT

The poem indicates some of the ways in which we link identity to place and the criteria which are used for making those connections. As we saw in Section 3.2, in everyday interactions we interpret the clues which are *given* and *given off* and classify people accordingly. For many of us it is no longer possible to 'read off' identity from the same signals we might have used in the past. This poem represents a contemporary question about identity. In attempting to classify people according to where they come from we may be thrown, when there are contradictory messages given off.

In this situation it is suggested that the white woman is confused by Kay's claims to be 'from Glasgow' because she apparently feels that black people cannot be 'really' Scottish (or British). The poem describes how the white woman here ignores the replies (and Kay's Glaswegian accent presumably) and insists that to be black is to be an outsider.

The poem also highlights the way in which identity is marked by **difference**. We have already seen that people mark their identities by some symbols of difference – scarves, badges, clothes, ways of speaking. This time the difference suggests that the white woman defines Kay as an outsider, in an *unequal* relationship of 'us and them'. 'Us' includes people who are the same as us, using the criteria which we think mark us out as the same, for example being white; 'them' are marked out as different because 'they' are not the same as 'us'. This suggests that 'we British' could be a superior category to 'those foreigners'. The key point about difference in the example of the poem is that being black or white is not only a way of marking difference but is used as a means of asserting superiority. Such assertions of superiority and the attempt to exclude people on grounds of 'race' and ethnicity can be described as racist.

Difference
Difference is relational. It has to be defined in relation to something else. For example, Monday is the day after Sunday and the day before Tuesday. Difference often involves oppositions which are unequal.

This poem is also about a search for certainty and disquiet about uncertainty. When 'snookered' by her earlier questions the white woman resorts to questions about 'purity'. She is seeking to locate identity in a category which we can mark off as fixed and certain. Kay's response to the misconceptions of the white woman is to deny any uncertainty on her own part. She gives voice to a collective identity which has meaning for her as an individual. She may be unclear about where she 'comes from' but is quite certain about who she is, who she wants to be and with whom she belongs. In her response Kay is offering one possible solution to the uncertainties posed by the question 'where do you come from?' in a multicultural and multi-ethnic society.

Multi-ethnicity and cultural diversity arising from the cultural differences in the contemporary UK raise a number of questions about uncertainty and diversity and about the ways in which people have the possibility, or not, of constructing their own identities. How can people respond so that they can actively engage with shaping their own identities? What kind of action is appropriate and how do we resolve the dilemmas with which we are presented? One strategy is to assert and celebrate difference as Kay does in her poem, in order to take control of her own identity. We have already seen unequal power relations, especially in the context of economic factors, as in our example of coal-mining. In this example, we see the social constraints which can operate through racist practices and ideas.

SUMMARY

- Identity is based on being the same as some people and different from others.
- Identities are constructed in relation to place.
- Difference is unequally weighted and can create categories of outsiders.
- Individuals and groups have to negotiate both the uncertainties of social change and the constraints of inequality.

Next we turn to another question which we might ask when we want to know more about someone. This time it suggests that people might have more control over their own identities.

8 WHO DO YOU WANT TO BE?

New social movements
Protest groups that challenged traditional politics and made identity a key factor in political mobilization.

It is not only through individual engagement that people seek to exercise agency and to forge new identities. The advent of new social movements in the West in the 1960s indicated collective endeavours to shape and give voice to new identities. These movements challenged traditional constraints and sought to celebrate a group's positive features as well as to challenge oppression. For example, the women's movement, the black civil rights movement, gay and lesbian rights movements, and the peace movement all sought actively to redefine the identities of their members. Campaigns around environmentalism, the politics of HIV and AIDS and for the rights of people with disabilities have challenged the idea that identities are fixed and cannot be reconstructed. The political projects of these group activities asserted collective identities. They also involve appeals to a certainty upon which the identities are based. For example, some gay rights activists have argued that their sexual identity is grounded in their biological make-up and is not a product of social processes. Some feminists have argued that women are intrinsically more peace-loving than men and that women have essential, female qualities which are superior to male aggression and should be celebrated as such – for example, as in the Greenham Common peace campaign.

FIGURE 1.7 Newbury Bypass protesters

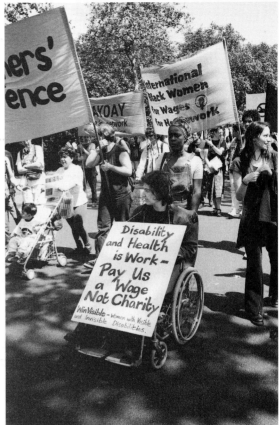

FIGURE 1.8 Campaigning for rights for carers

FIGURE 1.9
Gay rights
protestors

One of the concerns of *new social movements* has been to make us think in different ways about traditional ideas. Through collective action the word *gay* became a more positive representation of a sexual identity. Such social movements attempt to subvert stereotypes, shape new identities and celebrate diversity.

8.1 Body projects

In contemporary society the body has become a project. People attempt to alter or improve the appearance, size and shape of their bodies in line with their own designs. Think about the situations where this might happen: some people train at the gym or decorate their bodies with tattoos or even alter the appearance of their bodies through plastic surgery, such as face-lifts, liposuction and breast implants. Such body projects have become a feature of contemporary society, perhaps because of the consciousness people have of the inescapable reality of death: bodies age, become infirm and are subject to illness and disease. Body-building and boxing are examples of projects which challenge accepted notions of what is natural, especially when it is women who are involved in the activity. This can be seen as a form of resistance to constraining stereotypes of femininity.

ACTIVITY 1.4

Look at Figures 1.10 and 1.11.

How important are the constraints of the body and of biology here?

What do these pictures tell us about the ways in which it is possible to assert an identity through the body?

FIGURE 1.10   A woman body-builder demonstrates posing

FIGURE 1.11   The boxer Jane Couch training

COMMENT —————————————————————————

Arguments about what is 'natural' and about biology have been used to justify women's exclusion from particular activities. The women in these pictures can be seen as exercising agency to develop a particular kind of body which challenges cultural stereotypes. They are challenging what is thought appropriate gender behaviour. This illustrates one of the ways in which people use the body as a site for the construction of identity. Sometimes people engage in body projects which conform to existing stereotypes, but sometimes, as here, they assert resistance and create new identities. The body itself clearly offers some restrictions on what it is possible to do, but it is often difficult to disentangle what is biological and what is cultural. This is because we represent ourselves through the body itself as well as through what we wear. Sometimes campaigning groups which seek to present more positive images of themselves and to represent their collective identities do so through reconstructing the body and its images and challenging traditional expectations.

ACTIVITY 1.5

Look at the poster in Figure 1.12.

FIGURE 1.12   Hello boys?

Without looking at the words on the poster, what is the first thing you notice?

What is the stereotype which this image is designed to subvert?

C O M M E N T

Age Concern used this picture of 56-year-old Pearl Read, posing in the style of Eva Herzigova in the Wonder Bra advertisements featured on hoardings across the UK in the late 1990s, to challenge the expectation that 'older' people are unattractive and not sexually attractive. We may be more familiar with representations of young women as in, for example, the original Wonder Bra 'Hello boys' advertisement. This illustrates the importance of *representations* in the construction of identities. The most obvious representation in the above image is the association of sex and sexuality with provocative underwear. The item of clothing itself does not carry this meaning – it is the *association* which conveys it. In a women's changing room it would have a different meaning. Sexuality is one of the most frequent associations used in the promotion of commodities – for example, in car advertisements which include attractive and scantily dressed women. Meanings depend on the relationship between objects in the world and how we make sense of them in our heads. Words and images act as signs which express meaning but the meanings change according to the situation. This poster is a good example of the way in which symbols, often the same symbol, can be used to produce different meanings. In the original Wonder Bra advertisement, the message conveyed through the meaning of the symbol is sexual attractiveness and the promotion of the product by interpellating the would-be attractive woman purchaser. In the Age Concern poster, the pose and the look are used to symbolize a challenge to ageism and the constraints of stereotyping people according to their age.

One of the certainties which would appear to be offered by biology is that the human body declines in capabilities and attractiveness with age and eventually dies. What this poster does is to indicate the social meanings which are attached to the biological body. It presents a more complex view of ageing which suggests we as individuals might have some *control* over the process and especially the meanings associated with it.

SUMMARY

- Individuals and groups seek to challenge social expectations about identity.

- Through collective action and through individual projects people resist dominant cultural representations of identity.

- We can look in detail at how representations are produced and the role they play in the formation of identity.

9 CONCLUSION

Are we now better equipped to answer the three questions posed in the introduction?

How are identities formed?

We present ourselves to others through everyday interactions, through the way we speak and dress, marking ourselves as the same as those with whom we share an identity and different from those with whom we do not. Symbols and representations are important in the marking of difference and in both presenting ourselves to others and in visualizing or imagining who we are. We use symbols in order to make sense of ourselves in relation to the world we inhabit. This world is characterized by structures which may limit our choices, but which may also provide more opportunities.

How much constraint is exercised by social structures and how much control do we have in shaping our own identities?

Both as individuals and through collective action it is possible to redefine and reconstruct our identities. We can negotiate and interpret the roles we adopt. Through collective action it is also possible to influence the social structures which constrain us, but there are clearly restrictions and limits. The scripts of our everyday interactions are already written and at the wider level structures are deeply embedded in contemporary culture, economy and society. Identity formation continues to illustrate the interrelationship between structure and agency.

Is there more uncertainty about 'who we are' in the contemporary UK?

There have been changes in our lives, in the domestic arena, in the workplace, in our communities and at the level of the nation and its place in the world. Some of these changes have been translated into questions of identity, for example in concerns about how people cope with change. Change has also created new opportunities for redefining ourselves, at home and in the workplace and as members of different ethnicities and nations within the UK. There is both uncertainty and diversity. Identity is a particularly useful concept for explaining how people cope with change and uncertainty and the opportunities presented by diversity. Identities are fluid and changing. This, in itself, produces uncertainties.

This chapter has introduced not only some concepts and theories used by social scientists but also some of the ways in which they approach their task. We have started with *questions* and some tentative *claims*. What is happening to identities? How are they formed? Having offered some *definitions* which included the marking of difference and similarity and the link between the personal and the social, we then went on to find some *evidence*. Some of the evidence suggested that we know about the marking of difference through symbols and representation, which itself suggested *more questions* about how these symbols work. Could they work at the level of the unconscious? In order to explore further the link between the personal and the social we read an autobiographical account, another piece of evidence to which we applied some of the concepts about social structures which had been introduced earlier. This chapter has only introduced these ideas of social scientists starting with a question, seeking evidence and using concepts and theories to begin to offer an explanation. At each stage new questions emerge. The remaining chapters of this book extend this process, focusing on specific dimensions of identity. In Chapter 2 we look at something which might appear to be grounded in biology, gendered identities. In Chapter 3 we focus on the economic bases of identity, and in Chapter 4, using the examples of 'race' and ethnicity, we explore further social structures and the role of culture in shaping identities. The questions which were posed at the outset in this chapter and to which we have returned will inform the rest of the book so that we can produce a more complex picture of how identities are formed, the link between the personal and the social, the tension and relationship between structure and agency, and the degree to which identities are formed at a time of uncertainty which also offers diversity and opportunity for change.

REFERENCES

Althusser, L. (1971) *Lenin and Philosophy, and Other Essays*, London, New Left Books.

Bocock, R. (1983) *Sigmund Freud*, London, Tavistock.

Equal Opportunities Commission (1981) *Annual Report*.

Giddens, A. (1991) *Modernity and Self-Identity: Self and Society in the Late Modern Age*, Cambridge, Polity.

Goffman, E. (1959) *The Presentation of Self in Everyday Life*, New York, Doubleday Anchor.

Ignatieff, M. (1993) *Blood and Belonging: Journeys into the New Nationalism*, London, Chatto and Windus.

Kay, J. (1991) *A Dangerous Knowing*, London, Sheba.

Mead, G.H. (1934) *Mind, Self and Society*, Chicago, University of Chicago Press.

Mercer, K. (1990) 'Welcome to the Jungle' in Rutherford, J. (ed.) *Identity: Community, Culture, Difference*, London, Lawrence & Wishart.

Mooney, G., Kelly, B., Goldblatt, D. and Hughes, G. (2004) DD100 *Introductory Chapter. Tales of Fear and Fascination: The Crime Problem in the Contemporary UK*, Milton Keynes, The Open University.

Pateman, C. (1992) 'The patriarchal welfare state' in McDowell, L. and Pringle, R. (eds) *Defining Women*, Cambridge, Polity.

Social Trends, London, The Stationery Office for Office for National Statistics (annual).

Sarup, M. (1996) *Identity, Culture and the Postmodern World*, Edinburgh, Edinburgh University Press.

Williamson, J. (1986) *Consuming Passions*, London, Marion Boyars.

FURTHER READING

Richard Jenkins (1996) *Social Identity*, London, Routledge. This is an accessible introduction to debates about social identity which draws mainly on the disciplines of sociology and anthropology. It offers a well-illustrated discussion which elaborates the theories introduced in this chapter.

Madan Sarup (1996) *Identity, Culture and the Postmodern World*, Edinburgh, Edinburgh University Press. This book integrates social science material on identity with personal narrative about events in the author's autobiography. He provides accessible coverage of a range of approaches to identity with a focus on culture and representation.

Kath Woodward (2002) *Understanding Identity*, London, Arnold. This book maps out a range of theoretical debates about the concept of identity, linking them to contemporary issues and recent discussion about the importance of identity. Recent concerns, drawing on a wide range of examples, are located within historical debates.

Identity and gender

Jennifer Gove and Stuart Watt

Contents

1 INTRODUCTION

In this chapter, we are going to focus on an important dimension of identity, gender, and look at two significant claims about the way identity is constructed. First, we are going to investigate Kath Woodward's claim in the previous chapter, that gender identities are shaped by many different factors: individual and collective; biological and social. We are going to suggest that gender illuminates the complex multiple origins and practices of identity very clearly, because it allows us to explore our capacity for agency, and the social and biological structures that constrain our freedom to choose our gender identities.

In practice, biological and social differences between women and men are sufficiently important that we often use different words to describe them. This distinction between **sex** and **gender** is sometimes a very useful tool in the social sciences, because it allows us to concentrate on social differences between women and men, without worrying too much about biological differences. The problem with this distinction is that often biological and social influences are very tangled. Woodward's passport example clearly shows this tangling. Official documents do not actually use the word 'gender'; they use the word 'sex' instead, and everyone is categorized as either male or female. Many official documents, such as passports, birth certificates and death certificates, record sex explicitly. Many social scientists prefer to use the term gender to describe this area of difference, as it encompasses cultural and social practices *and* the bodies we inhabit. The use of the word gender suggests interconnections between culture and the body, rather than asserting a distinct separation between sex and gender, which is difficult and unrealistic to sustain.

Our second claim is that the way we construct our identities is strongly influenced by a set of often rather stereotypically **feminine** and **masculine** characteristics and traits that we often associate with gender categories, with women and with men. But women and men are not each made from a single mould. There are many different kinds of women and men, and different traits may apply to some more than to others. Behind the apparent simplicity of two genders, there is a diversity of gender characteristics, and many different influences are at work.

All societies have ways of differentiating between women and men, and between femininity and masculinity. These differences are often expressed through stereotypical language, through words which are associated with women and with men. The activity which follows includes some examples of this kind of language.

Sex
Sex is a biological classification.

Gender
Gender includes the social attributes associated with being a woman or a man in a particular society.

Feminine and masculine
Terms which are applied to the qualities particular societies associate with women and men.

ACTIVITY 2.1

Let's look at some of these stereotypical characteristics. Table 2.1 contains 45 different terms which might be used to describe people. Which, if any, of these words would you apply to yourself?

Reflect on the terms that you have chosen, and what they say about your identity. Do you think you are typically masculine or feminine?

TABLE 2.1   Some words that could be typical of one gender or another

tall	tender	arrogant
lucky	active	jealous
humane	proud	individualistic
tactful	modest	commanding
athletic	intuitive	unpretentious
weak	kind	passive
benevolent	decisive	conventional
assertive	unfriendly	strong
irresponsible	tidy	co-operative
perceptive	playful	robust
anxious	unemotional	reponsive
gentle	informal	flexible
vulnerable	calm	acute
dignified	vigorous	cheerful
crude	faithful	timid

Your responses will vary according to how you see yourself and the culture you are from. However, as we have seen, how you see yourself is only one part of identity. Now let's look more at the social side of identity, and consider how these different traits might be categorized by society as a whole, so that some are associated with men and others with women.

ACTIVITY 2.2

Look through the list of character descriptions in Table 2.1 again. For each one, write down whether you think it is thought to be typical of men or women in general, or neither, in your culture today.

COMMENT _____

Table 2.2 shows a gendered categorization of these traits, based on a small survey which we carried out in the UK. This shows how they can be regarded as culturally typical of women and of men in a particular society. Look again at your answers to Activities 2.1 and 2.2 in the light of this possible classification. There is clearly scope for disagreement here. Look specifically for differences between this classification and your answers, and think about why these differences might exist.

TABLE 2.2   Typically feminine and typically masculine characteristics

Feminine characteristics	Masculine characteristics	Neutral characteristics
anxious	active	acute
co-operative	arrogant	benevolent
faithful	assertive	calm
gentle	athletic	cheerful
humane	commanding	conventional
intuitive	crude	dignified
kind	decisive	flexible
passive	individualistic	informal
perceptive	irresponsible	jealous
responsible	proud	lucky
tactful	robust	modest
tender	strong	playful
tidy	tall	unfriendly
timid	unemotional	unpretentious
vulnerable	vigorous	weak

Categorizations like these reveal some aspects of how society and culture describe, and prescribe, gender-appropriate behaviours, qualities, and characteristics. These categories are not only the product of everyday exchanges; they can even be used in psychological testing, to classify and to measure the way we see ourselves.

How then can we use categorization to explore our two claims – the multiple sources of gender identity and the role of gender stereotypes?

In this chapter, we begin by looking at one theory of identity formation: *self-categorization theory*. Then, in Section 3, we will look at the development of gender identity in children, and in Section 4 we will look at the effects of gender identity on school performance.

SUMMARY

- Gender is a key dimension of identity.
- Gender identity is influenced by individual and collective and social and biological factors.
- Gender identities are often associated with stereotypically feminine and masculine traits.

2 GENDER IDENTITY AND SELF-CATEGORIZATION

Where does identity, and gender identity in particular, actually come from? We are going to focus on one account of the origins of gender identity by Turner and his colleagues (Turner *et al.*, 1987) called *self-categorization theory*. This explanation is rather like Althusser's concept of *interpellation*, described by Woodward in Chapter 1, Section 4.1.

In Althusser's account of identity, people are interpellated, or hailed, when they see a representation of a category and think, 'yes, that's me'. Look at Figure 1.2 in Section 4.1 of Chapter 1. Quite literally, people were encouraged to *identify* with representations like this. Advertisements do this quite explicitly sometimes, although at other times the process may be more subtle. These representations connect individuals to groups, and by becoming members of groups individuals take on new identities. The word 'identify' is telling: it signifies that the relationship between the individual and the representation has an emotional quality, an 'empathy', as well as a feeling of sameness. This is important to identity; it has a real feeling of personal involvement. Identity matters, at a personal level as well as a social one.

2.1 Explaining identity: self-categorization theory

Turner and his colleagues' theory claims that identity is shaped by self-categorization; by people looking at social categories, and deciding whether or not they are in a category. If they consider themselves a member of a category, that category becomes part of their identity. The explanation given by Turner's self-categorization theory works like this:

1 We see people as members of social categories.

2 We also see ourselves as members of social categories.

3 We take on identities appropriate to the social categories with which we identify.

Identity, then, includes people's notions of who they are, of what kind of people they are, and their relationships with others. It is therefore closely related to the *groups* – the social categories – that they see themselves as belonging to. So, for example, if Chris has an identity as a woman, this means that (a) she sees people divided into gender categories of women and men, and (b) she sees herself more as a member of the category of women.

Turner and his colleagues claim that similarity and difference influence self-categorization, and therefore identity. In effect, people are more likely to identify with a category they are similar to, compared with a category that is more different. The more different the person in the image is from you, the less likely you are to identify with it. Women would have been more likely to identify with the image in Figure 1.2 in Chapter 1 than men were.

So far, we have said very little about how gender categories actually work. We know that we refer to them using words like 'women' and 'men'. And to some extent we know what is going on inside them: we know there are traditionally feminine and masculine characteristics associated with each category, although these may vary between times and cultures. But to understand Turner's explanation properly, we need to be clearer about how we decide which gender category someone is in? This is central to steps 1 and 2 of Turner's explanation.

Let's look at an example of this happening in practice. What happens when a child is born? What category, *male* or *female*, will be written on their birth certificate? And what factors, biological or social, influence this categorization?

2.2 Gender categories: 'Is it a boy, or is it a girl?'

Lord Melchett   The whisper on the underground grapevine, ma'am, is that Lord Blackadder is spending all his time with a young boy in his service.

Queen Elizabeth I   Oh. Do you think he'd spend more time with me if I was a boy?

Lord Melchett   Surely not, ma'am.

Nursie   You almost were a boy, my little cherry pip.

Queen Elizabeth I   What?

Nursie   Yeah. Out you popped from your mummy's tumkin and everyone shouted, 'It's a boy! It's a boy!' And then someone said 'But it hasn't got a winkle!' And then I said, 'A boy without a winkle! God be praised – it's a miracle! A boy without a winkle!' And then Sir Thomas More pointed out that a boy without a winkle is a girl, and everyone was really disappointed.

Lord Melchett   Yes, well, you see he was a very perceptive man, Sir Thomas More.

Source: Elton and Curtis, 1998, pp.123–4

In the days of Queen Elizabeth I, practically the only significant factor which decided at birth whether the child was a girl or boy was the appearance of their genitalia – in effect, whether or not they had a 'winkle'. In this respect little has changed since then. Children are put into one of two categories according to these physical characteristics at birth. But is this really enough to define someone's gender? For Freud, as discussed in Chapter 1, Section 3.3, it was certainly very important. A child's psycho-sexual development depends on identifying with others of the same sex – and in this, Freud's explanation of gender relates to a child's self-categorization. And Freud, like Sir Thomas More, thought that girls' gender was significantly formed by the *absence* of a penis. This is illustrative of unequal power relations between the genders; the anatomical evidence is being used to reinforce a distinction that matters to society.

There is another problem with using anatomical evidence to define gender. In society, we usually wear clothes that hide a lot of our bodies. While for the most part we do not reveal our genitalia to people we meet casually, we usually have little problem deciding whether they are men or women. Because people usually wear clothes which present gender cues, social evidence is complicated by bodily evidence. Furthermore, because of the clothes, we can't usually see the anatomical evidence to help us tell the difference between women and men. So are there any other, more reliable, sources of evidence that we could use instead, to tell the difference between the gender categories?

"OH! THAT EXPLAINS THE DIFFERENCE IN OUR PAY"

© LEEDSpostcards

A second possible way to tell the difference between men and women is to use genetic evidence. Inside every cell in the human body is a number of long strings of the chemical DNA, called chromosomes. Of these, two, called the X and Y chromosomes, are called sex chromosomes. Generally speaking, humans either have two X chromosomes (and develop physically as women) or one X and one Y chromosome (and develop physically as men). So instead of checking for physical differences, we could use the genetic difference between women and men to define sex.

But there are problems with using genetic evidence to decide who should go into which category, just as there was with the bodily anatomical evidence. This time, it is the occasionally blurred boundary between the categories that shows the problem most clearly. Very rarely, people have more than two sex chromosomes; for example, people may have two Xs and one Y. But because females usually have two Xs, and males an X and a Y, these genetic intermediates could be categorized either way. Physically, too, they may have a mixture of bodily characteristics that makes categorization less certain than usual.

One solution to this problem is to define the categories more precisely. For example, Connell (1987) gives the example of the International Olympic Committee which decided simply to *define* all people with an intermediate pattern of chromosomes as men, so regardless of physical appearance they would not be allowed to participate in women's events. To categorize people at the Olympic Games, genetic tests are used, rather than physical checks. But this definition was made by a committee to maintain the status of the Games. The decision to use genetic evidence to define the categorization was made by a controlling social group. This has created problems for the individuals concerned, who suddenly find themselves re-categorized. Once again, biology does not give us a complete explanation of gender difference. Neither bodily nor genetic differences work all the time. Is there anywhere else we can look for a more certain account of the gender difference?

Another possibility is to argue that the difference between boys and girls is socially constructed. One hint of this is in the birth certificate itself. After birth, it is the birth certificate itself that defines sex, at least in the UK. Although the sex written on the certificate is based on biological evidence about our bodies at birth, and this evidence is assessed by a (presumably expert) doctor before being written into the formal certificate, the birth certificate then takes on a life of its own. It is this document that counts for

FIGURE 2.1   Official proof that we exist?

getting passports, citizenship, marriage, and so on; the original bodily evidence then becomes more or less irrelevant. To get a passport, or to get married, you do not need to display your genitalia.

So wherever we look we find that social and biological influences are tangled. At the bodily level, and at the genetic level, there are social influences at work, and at the social level there are biological influences at work. Many factors contribute to defining gender: the way we dress and cut our hair, the genetic information inside our cells, and the form of our bodies. No single set of these defines, unambiguously, whether we are men or women.

Something else about the gender categories may have struck you. Why are there two categories? Why are there not many more categories to cover the diversity of experience? Why are people not all in one gender category? After all, the differences between men and women are pretty small compared with the similarities between them. This is a tricky issue, which we will come back to in Section 3, but remember what Woodward said in the previous chapter: *identity is marked by difference*. Categories, such as gender categories, can reflect an *unequal* relationship of *us* (those inside the category) and *them* (those outside, in a different category). The differences between us as individuals are reduced compared with the larger differences between *us* and *them*. In other words, without difference, there could not be such a thing as identity; without a *them* there could never be an *us*. Categories, such as the gender categories that we have investigated, are organized into systems which make 'us and them' possible.

2.3 Are we free to change our gender identity?

In current UK law, even if bodily evidence is changed, there is as yet no way for a person's legal sex to be changed accordingly. This is because, in the UK, someone's legal sex is defined by the sex assigned at birth. What is commonly called a 'sex change' operation (more correctly known as 'gender reassignment') does not affect a person's legal sex, and they can still only legally marry someone of the opposite sex to that on their birth certificate. Although someone may adopt a new gender by changing their clothes, their behaviour, and even their body, the birth certificate constrains their use of the new gender. The birth certificate takes the uncertainties of gender, and hides them as far as the law is concerned. In the UK, people are not completely free to choose their gender identity.

There are two stories we can tell about what defines gender categories. According to the first story, there is an *essence* to a category, which things have if they are in the category, and do not have if they are not in the category. Having a penis, or having a Y chromosome, are good examples of this kind of essence to the category 'male'. This story about categories is

[handwritten margin note:] You can take all the characteristics of new gender but legally their birth certificate constrain their use of their new gender.

Essentialist
This viewpoint regards, say, having a Y chromosome as essential to being a male and reduces gender to one factor. An account of identity in general and gender identity in particular which reduces gender to possession of a single characteristic or essence.

called **essentialist**, because it regards, say, having a Y chromosome, as essential to being male and reduces gender to one factor. All other gender characteristics, such as those categorized as masculine in Table 2.2 above, would simply be consequences of having this essence. However, as we discussed earlier, there do not seem to be any essential characteristics, at either the bodily, genetic, or social level, that unambiguously decide gender category membership.

In the second story, there are no clear criteria as to whether or not something is in the category. Instead, the category is rather fuzzy. Although most of the cases may be really clear, there are a few unclear cases around the edges. This story about categories is non-essentialist, simply because there is no essence to the category; many factors contribute to the gender categories. As we have seen, gender categories seem to be non-essentialist in character.

Essentialist categories claim to be clear and immutable, so they tend to remain fixed. Fuzzy categories, on the other hand, can and do drift a bit, so what it is to be a woman, or man, may vary as times and cultures change.

2.4 Gender stereotypes

Essentialist categories have important consequences. Essences are all or nothing – you are either in the category or outside it, but there is no in-between. With non-essentialist categories, you can be more or less in the category. There is a lot more room for diversity. People can be more or less typical representatives of the gender categories that they belong to. There are many kinds of men and women – typical men and atypical men, and similarly typical women and atypical women, rather than just men and women – although what counts as typical will vary between cultures. Typical men, for example, might have most of the characteristics that we would expect of 'men in general'. Atypical men have rather fewer of the characteristics we might expect; they might, for example, be bored by sport on television, not have a car to wash on Sunday afternoons, or they might enjoy doing the washing up.

Typicality, as we have cast it, looks a bit like masculinity or femininity. Is this the case? Where do these 'typical' features that we associate with gender categories come from? Look back at Figure 1.2 in Chapter 1. This image is interesting because it represents a stereotype of femininity at a particular time. A **stereotype** is a simplified, and possibly exaggerated, representation of the most common typical characteristics associated with a category. Despite the fact that it may be biased, it often, although not always, has a grain of truth (look at your responses to Activities 2.1 and 2.2 if you are not convinced). Stereotypes are usually either positively or negatively biased, although different people may hold very differently valued stereotypes. Positive stereotypes, such as the image of the pregnant woman in the workplace in Figure 1.3 in the previous chapter, often encourage identification. Negative

Stereotype
A simplified representation of the most typical characteristics associated with a category.

stereotypes, on the other hand, are associated with prejudice. The word 'prejudice' means judging people *before* you have met them, and this is exactly how both positive and negative stereotypes work, although they may continue to influence our perceptions afterwards for good and for ill.

This link with identification is important, as it suggests that stereotypes – particularly positive stereotypes – are linked with identity. In fact, Turner and his colleagues' explanation makes a clear claim: that positive stereotypes are generally linked to, and defined by, the *in-group* (the one you are a member of) and negative stereotypes tend to be linked to, and defined by, the *out-group* (the one which is different, which you are not a member of). Because of this difference between the groups, the positive and negative stereotypes tend to reflect, and even reinforce, Woodward's unequal relationship of *us and them*.

2.5 Masculinities and femininities

Stereotypes do not just shape the way we perceive other people, they also shape the way we behave. People are active players in the development and construction of their own identities. People can, within limits, change themselves to fit their understanding and views of gender. As part of this, people often adopt gender-typical behaviour to form and fit with the identities that they construct. Identity is not just something we achieve, nor something that is just thrust upon us; it has elements of both.

Looking back at Activities 2.1 and 2.2, you should now find that categorization makes makes more sense of stereotypes. The characteristics in Tables 2.1 and 2.2 are illustrative of the gender stereotypes. But where did these characteristics come from?

We selected these characteristics by running a small experiment. We put together a big pool of possible traits, and presented it to a panel of judges. These judges were asked to rate each characteristic by how strongly gender-linked it was. We treated the judges not as giving a correct categorization, but simply as a window on to one particular culture – in this case, the UK in 1999. Other cultures are rather different, and times change, so there may be some significant differences between different cultures' interpretations of the traits in Table 2.1, and about what is considered gender-appropriate in a culture. Sandra Bem conducted a study in the USA in the 1970s (Bem, 1974). Her findings suggested that there were distinct and recognizable characteristics associated with femininity and masculinity in the USA at the time. There have been some shifts. Today, in the UK, it may be more acceptable for men to exhibit feminine traits, but in other ways not so much has changed.

Something else might have struck you about the character descriptions in Tables 2.1 and 2.2; the descriptions are not equally valued within a culture, although the characteristics that are most valued will vary between cultures.

For example, men are described as individualistic, assertive, and athletic, women as intuitive, perceptive, and tactful. Bem recognized this issue: in her study she interpreted the feminine and masculine, not as opposites, but as different dimensions, as shown in Figure 2.2. Bem considered it possible to be both masculine and feminine at the same time (she called this type of person 'androgynous'), or to be neither masculine nor feminine (she called this 'undifferentiated'). She wanted to abandon the common-sense opposition of feminine and masculine, and offer freedom for a greater diversity of masculinities and femininities, allowing both women and men to be free agents, able to take on the valued characteristics.

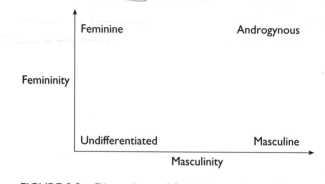

FIGURE 2.2   Dimensions of femininity and masculinity in Bem's Sex Role Inventory
Source: Turner, 1995, Figure 6, p.17

SUMMARY

- Turner and his colleagues use *self-categorization theory* as an account of identity, an account that links with Althusser's notion of interpellation.

- Self-categorization theory suggests that identity is shaped by the categories with which we label ourselves and identify.

- Gender categories show biological, social, and possibly even genetic, factors at work, but no clear single influence dominates.

- Gender categories are also associated with stereotypes, which may be either positive or negative, and which can reinforce the relationship of 'us and them'.

So far, we have looked in considerable detail at adults' gender categories, and at how they might work to shape the construction of our gender identities. In Section 3 we will explore how children construct and take on identities as they develop.

3 GENDER IDENTITY AND GENDER DEVELOPMENT

In this section we are going to look at where we come from in terms of childhood experience and the development of gender identities in childhood. We have already learned that gender identity involves the construction and use of gender categories. Children's gender categories are at first rather simplistic; but, as we shall see, children refine their categories so that they become more reliable and useful for their social lives. Studying the development of gender identity in children reveals that this is a story of a search for certainty. In Section 2 we discovered that self-categorization is a necessary part of developing a gender identity. In exploring the formation of gender identity in children it would therefore be sensible to ask questions about children's construction and use of gender categories.

We look at four key questions in this section:

- At what age do children display behaviour that suggests they are using gender categories?
- At what age can children categorize themselves (and others) as belonging to a gender category, and what does this categorization mean to them?
- Are young children's gender categories different from those of adults, and if so in what ways?
- How are gender identities maintained in later childhood?

What evidence exists about children's use of gender categories? Children's preference for particular toys is some of the earliest behaviour indicating a categorization of masculine and feminine. Preferences, behaviours or traits that

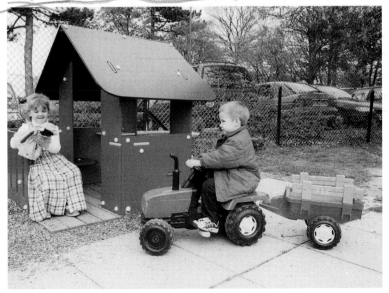

FIGURE 2.3   Some toys are considered to be appropriate for boys and others for girls

Gender-appropriate
Preferences, behaviours
or traits deemed to be
suitable or proper with
regard to masculinity
and femininity in a
particular culture.

mirror the views of one's society about what is masculine and what is feminine are termed **gender-appropriate**. Opting for gender-appropriate toys (masculine toys such as trucks, toolkits, and construction kits if one is a boy and feminine toys such as dolls, tea-sets, and domestic items if a girl) can usually be seen by 2 years of age. There is evidence that from 3 or 4 years, children are able to categorize toys as suitable for boys or girls, and knowledge of the gender-appropriateness of toys strongly influences preferences.

Our second question asked about children's ability to categorize themselves appropriately. Some researchers believe that consistent gender labelling is a particularly important milestone. Most children can categorize themselves appropriately and consistently as a boy or girl at some time between 2 and 3 years of age. Durkin (1995) describes this as a gradual process:

> ... the child slowly becomes aware that he or she is a member of a particular sex. At first, this knowledge constitutes little more than a label for the child, equivalent to a personal name. The child begins to discover which other individuals fall into the same category, and elaborates his or her gender labels to include terms such as man, woman, boy, girl. But knowledge is not perfect.
>
> (Durkin, 1995, p.180)

There is evidence that some important gender-appropriate behaviours result from the child's ability to categorize themselves as a boy or girl. Such behaviours include having a greater preference for same-gender peers. However, some gender-appropriate behaviours such as toy preference, as we have seen, occur before this milestone is typically reached. Once children are able to categorize themselves and others appropriately, they can draw upon (and build upon) their previously acquired knowledge to refine their construction of gender categories, and further develop their own sense of gender identity.

So from quite an early age children are able to categorize themselves as male or female. Perhaps this is early evidence of the formation of gender identity. What, though, does the label that children initially apply to themselves actually mean to them? What did Durkin (in the quotation above) mean when he noted that children's knowledge 'is not perfect'? The answer to these questions depends upon evidence relating to our third question about the development of gender identity. This question asked whether the gender categories used by young children differed from those of adults. Learning more about the characteristics of children's gender categories can tell us more about the sorts of gender identity they are forming.

Research has found that gender categories typically constructed by young children under about 5 years of age have particular and distinct characteristics (Kolhberg, 1966). The evidence for this is revealed through mistakes that children make. They may, for example, suggest that girls can become uncles, and boys become aunts. In addition to misunderstandings about the stability of gender over time, children are often also fooled by context. If outward appearances change, if, for example, a man dresses in woman's clothing, or if a man engages in activities considered to be typically feminine, then children may consider such a man to have changed into a woman.

Think back to Section 2 in which we discussed how categories can be constructed in different ways. What may the structure of young children's gender categories be like, such that they result in misunderstandings about gender?

Young children's gender categories are highly stereotyped. This can lead to assured predictions of an individual's preferences based upon knowledge of their gender, and the kinds of activities that they may typically engage in. Children develop such rigid gender categories in their search for certainty about gender. These categories are essentialist, having a simple in-group and out-group distinction that children use for understanding masculinity and femininity, and for defining their own gender identity. However, because the categories they use are inflexible, this leads them to make mistakes about gender. Given these distinctive characteristics of young children's gender categories, we can describe children as being *naïvely certain* about gender.

How might the construction of children's gender categories lead them to believe that gender may not be stable throughout life? Although a few people may change their gender identity, as adults we need a sophisticated understanding of this, rather than a naïve belief that when surface characteristics change (such as clothes and make-up) so does gender. Take a look at the quotation below:

Johnny (age $4\frac{1}{2}$) I'm going to be an airplane builder when I grow up.

Jimmy (age 4) When I grow up, I'll be a mommy.

Johnny No, you can't be a mommy. You have to be a daddy.

Jimmy No, I'm going to be a mommy.

Johnny No, you're not a girl, you can't be a mommy.

Jimmy Yes, I can.

Source: Kohlberg, 1966, p.95

Jimmy, although of an age where he can presumably label himself as a boy, believes that he can be a mommy when he grows up. The current construction of his own gender identity does not restrict him to remaining the same gender throughout life. Why might this be? Research conducted by Bem (1989), described in Box 2.1, illustrates that young children look for certainty in gender categories that they construct using *social* and *cultural* characteristics. Bem's study reveals that young children's categories are less influenced by *biological* knowledge, and this, claims Bem, is principally because they simply do not have this knowledge.

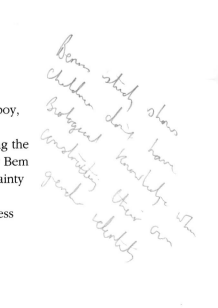

BOX 2.1 **What are young children's gender categories made of?**

In an experimental study, Bem (1989) found that only about half of 3, 4, and early 5-year-olds were able to draw upon biological knowledge (genitalia) in deciding whether pictures of nude toddlers were boys or girls. Most of the children who were successfully able to identify boys and girls from biological cues were subsequently able to categorize the same children consistently as boys or girls when they were shown pictures of them in clothes and with hairstyles characteristically associated with the opposite gender. In other words, most children who were able to categorize gender on the basis of biological cues were not swayed in their judgements by the contradictory gender-cues presented through surface appearances. Most of those children who could not correctly identify boys and girls from seeing their genitalia were more likely to decide the gender of the same child in subsequent pictures on the basis of appearance.

So early gender categorization is particularly dependent upon social and cultural experiences. Perhaps this can help us to understand why young children make mistakes about the stability and constancy of gender, and why their gender categories are defined in highly stereotypical ways. As adults, we know that just because someone changes appearance from one gender to another (for a fancy dress party, for example), or just because they engage in activities that are considered to be typically appropriate to the opposite gender, they nevertheless remain the same gender. This is because our understanding of gender embodies both biological and social knowledge – our understanding of gender is complex and sophisticated. We understand (unlike young children) that changing our gender identity takes more than changing our outward appearance or the activities that we do. In addition, we also understand that just because someone prefers woodwork, football, and beer over needlework, netball, and wine, it does not necessarily mean that person is a man. This is because we are aware that the links between our stereotypes do not correspond neatly to being a man or a woman; there is indeed diversity with regard to gender in our society. However, if we were made to place a bet about someone's gender given particular characteristics, we might draw upon our stereotypical knowledge in doing so; but stereotypes cannot be relied upon, and as adults we know this.

Multiple gender identities Masculinities and femininities, rather than one masculine and one feminine type. In any society there is a whole range of ways in which femininity and masculinity can be expressed.

Gradually, children's culturally defined gender categories are supplemented with biological knowledge. Children from about 5 years of age onwards learn that their own and others' gender identity generally remains the same across time and across contexts. This is a profound development in the gradual construction of gender identity. As the gender categories that children develop become more reliable, they also become more flexible and are no longer essentialist. Children learn that there are **multiple gender identities**, masculinities and femininities, rather than one masculine and one feminine type. Children are still certain about gender, just as we generally are as adults;

but this is now because, like adults' categories, their categories become more reliable and adaptive.

Although gender categories become more flexible, they continue to work as powerful social tools. The gender categories used in the construction of gender identity are actively maintained and re-constructed throughout our lives. But, as our fourth question asks, how does this come about? Francis (1997, 1998) has conducted some interesting research with school children, that examines the construction and maintenance of their gender identities. This research is described in Box 2.2.

BOX 2.2   **Gender identity and gender maintenance**

Francis (1997, 1998) asked primary school children (aged 7 to 11 years) to engage in some pretend role play. The groups of children were asked to choose between play situations of a hospital, hotel, or school, and they had to choose the roles that they were going to play from a set provided. Francis observed the children's play and examined their talk. In choosing their roles, boys took the high-status positions of doctor, manager and head teacher slightly more often than girls. Those boys taking high-status positions used their role to exert domination and power far more often than did girls.

The gender roles the boys took on and constructed could be described as 'typically masculine' and those of the girls as 'typically feminine'. Particularly when playing in mixed groups, the children constructed the gender roles as oppositional to each other. In general, Francis found that the girls took on sensible, selfless, mature, and facilitating behaviours, and boys took on silly, selfish, immature, and demanding behaviours. Such gender-typical behaviours correspond to previous research with school children which has consistently found girls at school to be diligent, sensible and quiet and boys to be rowdy, disruptive, and preoccupied with violence. Francis interprets the children's constructions of oppositional gender roles to be part of a process of identity maintenance.

Adoption of typical gender identities generated situations in the role play in which the girls (typically feminine) behaviours, such as willingly accepting low-status roles, and facilitating the role play with their sensible suggestions, supported the boys' (typically masculine) behaviours of taking up high-status roles and behaving in a demanding and selfish way. Francis notes how the girls' adoption of such feminine positions is simply demonstrative of socially appropriate feminine behaviour, which she describes as exemplifying a 'properly female' identity.

Francis is careful to point out that these gender-appropriate identities and behaviours were not taken up by all children; instead, they were fluid, and some children challenged or ignored them. Francis suggests that children work quite hard in constructing and maintaining their gender identities; but it also highlights that the behaviours typical of masculine and feminine roles are not binding, and that there is opportunity for diversity. Why are gender categories and gender identities not fixed? One reason, as Francis points out, is that gender constructions are only one part of our identities, alongside ethnicity and social class, for example. Sometimes the influences of these other factors may reinforce those of gender; at other times they may outweigh them, and this affords diversity. Because many factors interact in the construction of identity, there can be no single masculinity or femininity; there must instead be a diversity of masculinities and femininities.

This section has discussed the typical pattern of gender identity development and has shown that gender is crucial to identity and our understanding of who we are. But just as there is diversity in terms of masculinity and femininity, there is diversity too in children's acquisition of gender identity. Children have different experiences and develop at different rates. It is also important to note that research takes place at a particular time, and in a particular place, so the story of the typical may also be culturally biased.

SUMMARY

- Children's developing understanding of gender can be described as a search for certainty.

- Young children make mistakes about gender illustrating their rigidity and their naïve certainty regarding gender.

- As children's knowledge of gender grows in complexity, basic biological knowledge is added to their social–cultural understanding.

- Research by Francis illustrating girls' 'sensible-selfless' and boys' 'silly-selfish' behaviour demonstrates how gender identities are constructed and maintained.

- Children's knowledge of gender in relation to their own identity and that of others develops both in terms of flexibility (in that they can accommodate diversity) and in reliability.

- Masculine and feminine identities are not fixed, partly because identities are multidimensional. Diversity arises through the existence of masculinities and femininities.

We are going to continue to follow the story of what is typical through investigating how constructions and perceptions of gender identities may affect experience of school and subsequently performance at school. We will explore the claim that performance in exams may to a certain extent be dependent upon gender, both in terms of one's own identity, and in terms of how schooling as a social process deals with masculinity and femininity.

4 GENDER AND ACADEMIC ACHIEVEMENT

● ● ● ● ● ● ● ● ● ● ● ● ● ● ● ● ● ● ● ●

ACTIVITY 2.3

What do you recall about being at school? Note down your thoughts. The following questions may help you:

What did you do in the playground? If you played games, what were these?

What did you do in physical education lessons?

Did you participate in any out-of-school activities? What were these?

What were your favourite school subjects?

Which subjects were you good at and which were you bad at?

Can you see any patterns or themes in your answers?

Do you think that any of the activities you can remember doing were related to your gender?

COMMENT _____

People's experience of school differs greatly. Your reflections on gender differences in your school years may depend upon how long ago your schooling was, and the sort of school you went to. You may have attended a single-sex school; or perhaps, in your coeducational school, boys and girls were separated for some subjects, such as physical education. Your school's curriculum might have dictated different activities for boys and girls. Perhaps you can remember whether girls' or boys' names were called first when the register was taken, or whether where you sat in class depended upon gender. You may remember the sorts of subject you opted for, and how good you and others were at different subjects.

_____

There are clear patterns in the subjects that boys and girls take and do well at in school. For a long time in the UK boys were found to perform better than girls in science exams, and girls have outperformed boys in English. Such general trends cannot necessarily explain the performance of individuals. Indeed, the significant diversity in performance across gender should also be recognized. However, the strong statistical patterns in performance relating to gender that do exist are worthy of social scientific investigation.

4.1 'Boys performing badly'

In 1944, the Butler Education Act introduced a three-tiered system of schooling in England and Wales. Based upon results in the eleven-plus examination, pupils could attend either a grammar school, a boys' technical school (though there were fewer of these), or a secondary modern school. More grammar school places were made available for boys. This practice was justified on the basis of boys' 'later maturity'. Class was an issue of concern relating to this tripartite system, since the middle classes were disproportionately represented in grammar schools; but in general gender issues were not addressed. It was not until feminists raised the issue of gender inequalities in schooling during the 1960s and 1970s that gender, and particularly lack of opportunities for girls, linked up with political and research agendas. Until quite recently, concern has generally been focused on female underachievement. However, the latest trends, reported widely through the media, have shown girls out-achieving boys even in subjects traditionally considered as 'male', such as mathematics, science, and technology-based subjects, and the gap in achievement for English increasing. In the 1990s the statistics made the headlines, some of which can be seen in Figure 2.4.

Girls outclassing boys

The Guardian, 26 November 1997, p.1

Now boys' results give 'cause for concern'

TES, 5 December 1997, p.4

Girls really are better than boys – official

The Observer, 4 January 1998, p.1

Boys performing badly

The Observer, 4 January 1998, p.13

FIGURE 2.4
Newspaper headlines relating to changing patterns in examination results

Why do you think there has been such concern about boys' underachievement, but no such *moral panic* when girls were underachieving in mathematics and sciences in the 1950s and 1960s?

The poor performance of boys caused widespread concern which was unprecedented in relation to previous debates about gender and school achievement, which suggests a profound concern with boys' underachievement. The situation was declared a 'crisis' and the government requested action to address the problem from each education authority. It is not only Britain that has been experiencing this trend in the underachievement of boys compared with girls. Similar patterns can be found across a number of developed countries (Murphy and Elwood, 1998), as can the consequent alarm.

Let us have a look at the figures for the 1990s when these issues were first raised. Figure 2.5 displays the percentage of 16-year-old girls and boys in England achieving GCSE A*–C grades in (a) five or more subjects, (b) English, (c) Maths, (d) Science.

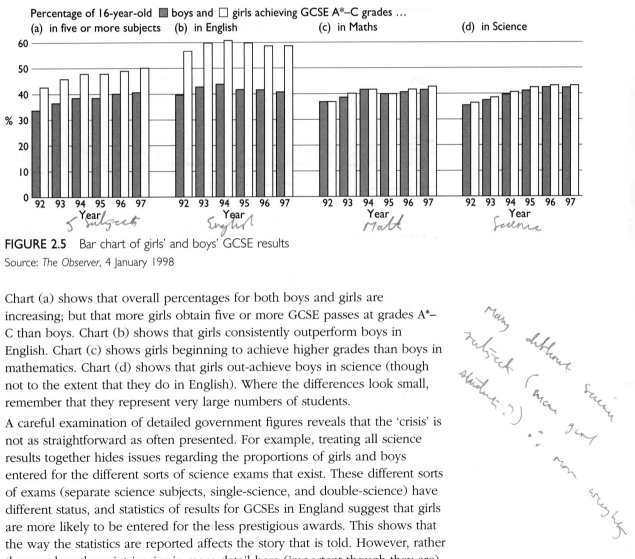

FIGURE 2.5 Bar chart of girls' and boys' GCSE results
Source: *The Observer*, 4 January 1998

Chart (a) shows that overall percentages for both boys and girls are increasing; but that more girls obtain five or more GCSE passes at grades A*–C than boys. Chart (b) shows that girls consistently outperform boys in English. Chart (c) shows girls beginning to achieve higher grades than boys in mathematics. Chart (d) shows that girls out-achieve boys in science (though not to the extent that they do in English). Where the differences look small, remember that they represent very large numbers of students.

A careful examination of detailed government figures reveals that the 'crisis' is not as straightforward as often presented. For example, treating all science results together hides issues regarding the proportions of girls and boys entered for the different sorts of science exams that exist. These different sorts of exams (separate science subjects, single-science, and double-science) have different status, and statistics of results for GCSEs in England suggest that girls are more likely to be entered for the less prestigious awards. This shows that the way the statistics are reported affects the story that is told. However, rather than explore these intricacies in more detail here (important though they are), we will turn our attention to reflecting upon *why* differences in performance may exist. We will consider whether differences are *natural*, to do with the biology of being male or female; and whether experiences of, and interactions with, social structures can account for differences found. In our consideration of social and cultural influences, we will also discuss the construction and assessment of the tests and exams upon which performance is based.

4.2 Exploring the origins of performance differences

Cognitive tests are designed to measure the ability to reason perceptually, mathematically, and linguistically. Results of such tests show that, although there is a great deal of similarity in the areas in which males and females both achieve, in general males do better on some sorts of tasks and females do better on others. Some examples of these tasks can be seen in Figure 2.6. The premise of such research is that differences found between large samples of males and females are *natural* and innate. Such research can be considered to be a search for certainty in relation to gender differences.

Researchers investigating the biology and physiology of brain structure and function suggest that cognitive specialization of males and females (for example, women tend to do better on verbal tests and men on spatial tests) may be due to organizational differences in the brain, or influences of early sex hormones (Kimura, 1992). However, it is very difficult to claim that cognitive testing can give a measure of *natural* ability, since lifestyle factors (the different experiences of men and women) can never really be excluded.

Criticisms of the tests themselves also challenge the claim that men and women have distinct problem-solving abilities. As Linda Birke points out, 'Tests may measure only a very limited range of appropriate skills; verbal skills, for example, include a wider range of abilities, such as reading, and may depend upon other abilities, such as reasoning' (1992, p.99). In addition, interpretation of the results can be problematic. Many test results show no or little difference between the performance of males and females, highlighting instead similarities in distributions of achievement, and such results often go unreported.

Birke raises a further concern about the relationship that is drawn between performance on cognitive tests and 'natural' biological predispositions. She writes, 'It is ... a strange kind of biology – for these theories portray the differences as somehow etched into a fixed kind of brain. Yet surely the human brain is anything but fixed: on the contrary, it shows amazing capacities for learning and memory' (1992, p.100). Birke questions the pursuit of certainty, and reliance on ideas of fixed differences between men and women. The differences found may result from a complex **interaction** between biology and social–cultural experiences: biological processes are responsive to environmental influences and vice versa. None the less, the view that cognitive strengths and weaknesses of men and women are 'determined' by an unalterable biology is pervasive.

Interaction
Biological processes are responsive to environmental influences and vice versa.

Problem-Solving Tasks Favoring Women

Women tend to perform better than men on tests of perceptual speed, in which subjects must rapidly identify matching items—for example, pairing the house on the far left with its twin:

In addition, women remember whether an object, or a series of objects, has been displaced:

On some tests of ideational fluency, for example, those in which subjects must list objects that are the same color, and on tests of verbal fluency, in which participants must list words that begin with the same letter, women also outperform men:

Women do better on precision manual tasks—that is, those involving fine-motor coordination—such as placing the pegs in holes on a board:

And women do better than men on mathematical calculation tests:

77	$14 \times 3 - 17 + 52$
43	$2(15+3) + 12 - \dfrac{15}{3}$

Problem-Solving Tasks Favoring Men

Men tend to perform better than women on certain spatial tasks. They do well on tests that involve mentally rotating an object or manipulating it in some fashion, such as imagining turning this three-dimensional object

or determining where the holes punched in a folded piece of paper will fall when the paper is unfolded:

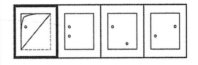

Men also are more accurate than women in target-directed motor skills, such as guiding or intercepting projectiles:

They do better on disembedding tests, in which they have to find a simple shape, such as the one on the left, once it is hidden within a more complex figure:

And men tend to do better than women on tests of mathematical reasoning:

1,100	If only 60 percent of seedlings will survive, how many must be planted to obtain 660 trees?

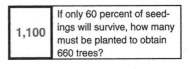

FIGURE 2.6

Cognitive testing: problem-solving tasks favouring women and men

Source: Kimura, 1992, pp.82 and 83

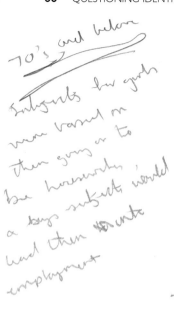

70's and before

Subjects for girls were based on women going on to be houseworks, boys subjects would lead then to write employment

Some of the criticisms that have been brought against cognitive tests can also be applied to school tests that have generated the recent 'crisis'. Birke raised the issue that tests sometimes do not actually measure what they are supposed to measure, or that they may only measure a highly restricted range of abilities. Psychologists describe this as a concern with the *validity* of the tests. This type of argument has also been made by feminist educationalists and applied to school testing. Ideas surrounding performance have been broadened and realized in the wider criteria for testing implemented through GCSE examinations; but despite the shift from testing knowledge of facts to testing the use of knowledge, tests and examinations still serve to define school achievement particularly narrowly. Another anxiety about the validity of cognitive tests was the likely, but often unacknowledged, influence of social and cultural factors. In short, perhaps boys and girls have different experiences inside and outside of school, which may explain the achievement patterns. Let us look at these experiences in more detail.

From the early 1970s, feminist studies have shown how women (in all sorts of contexts) are often considered the inferior 'Other'. Since the beginnings of formal education, women's education has been considered as secondary to men's, and the curriculum for women was shaped by beliefs about biology, the female body, and the services that women would consequently 'naturally' aspire to (Paechter, 1998). This is explored in Box 2.3.

| BOX 2.3 | **Educating the Other** |

Paechter (1998) in her book *Educating the Other* notes that in the nineteenth century there was:

> ... a concern to protect adolescent girls from 'mental overstrain' and it was believed that 'over-educated' women would be unable to breast-feed ... At the same time, it was this assumed future role of wife, and in particular, mother, that to a large extent shaped nineteenth and twentieth century girls' education.

(Paechter, 1998, p.12)

Further, she notes that at the beginning of the twentieth century:

> ... a girl might spend half of the time in her last year on domestic subjects. This of course led to the exclusion of other studies; boys were usually taught elementary arithmetic while the girls did needlework ... Both the elementary and secondary curricula for girls emphasised an ideology of service; this persists up to the present day, inscribed in the practices not only of food and textile technology ... but also of business subjects ... Summerfield (1987) argues that schools still teach girls that their main objective is preparation for a caring role, both in the home and at work, so girls are encouraged to regard themselves as secondary, servicing, Other to men.

(Paecher, 1998, p.13)

Education has had, and still has, a particular purpose for girls that is different from and inferior to that for boys. It claims that the different experiences of girls and boys shape identities in specific ways. Of course, there have been many changes both inside and outside school since the beginnings of formal education.

Can you think of any changes with regard to gender identity and gender roles within educational establishments since you were at school?

If you have only recently left school, try to think of changes since you started school.

Changes in social structures may contribute to shifts in attitudes, and the construction of new, though perhaps still distinctive, masculine and feminine identities at school. Although the research evidence is not conclusive, economic and labour market changes may be playing some part in shaping the attitudes and self-perceptions of particular groups of boys and girls and influencing their behaviour in school. There may therefore be at least an indirect effect on performance.

Whilst there is much debate about whether there are increasing opportunities for women to take higher status managerial positions, or whether the *glass ceiling* is just as resilient as ever, the proportion of women in such jobs has increased. At the same time, uncertainty has been experienced by many men in regions where traditional apprenticeships and other routes for boys into the labour market have been in sharp decline. A number of research studies have suggested that this rather dramatic labour market shift has perpetuated a particular youth sub-culture – 'the macho lads', who, with no potential for achievement in terms of working-class male craftsmanship, do not identify with schooling. They seek alternative anti-school values and adopt 'laddish' attitudes and behaviour (Mac an Ghaill, 1994). This may be a result of societal changes challenging traditional gender identities. The newspaper comment and discussion headlines shown in Figure 2.7 suggest that it is the attitudes, values and identities of these boys that underpin poor achievement patterns.

Other evidence suggests that the notion of achieving academically is now broadly linked with femininity, and that this is shunned by some boys in the construction and expression of their masculine identities. The current experiences of boys suggest that it is 'uncool' to be seen to be a high achiever and that one must at all costs avoid gaining the identity of a 'boffin'. In fact, cultivating an identity that will be accepted by peers in school may require the careful adoption of particular behaviours:

> I get a bit of stick myself because I really like English. Sometimes I don't bother answering or asking questions in class because I will worry that my friends will take the mickey out of me for being teacher's pet.
>
> (Daniel, aged 13, quoted in *The Guardian*, 6 January 1998, p.6)

> In the year above me there's a boy who wears five merit badges and he gets stick off everyone. I've got two, but I only wear one.
>
> (Sam, aged 13, quoted in *The Observer*, 4 January 1998, p.13)

How to turn the new lads into new men
The Guardian, Education, 13 January 1998, pp.2–3

Learning gender gap reveals redundant male
The Observer, 4 January 1998, p.19

A bad way to educate boys

The Independent, Education+, 3 April 1997, p.8

Problems that arise when boys will be lads
The Guardian, 6 January 1998, p.6

Boys turned off by homework

TES Scotland, 23 January 1998, p.3

FIGURE 2.7 Newspaper discussion headlines relating achievement and male identities

Particular aspects of typically masculine and typically feminine identities relate to specific school-based activities and to achievement. One much publicized example is that of reading, often commonly considered to be a feminine interest, and more often recognized as part of feminine rather than masculine identities. Note Daniel's reflection on his peers' reaction to his enjoyment of English, as reported in the above quotation from *The Guardian*.

Whilst there is much concern about boys' poor levels of literacy, and the increasing gender gap evident in English examinations, it is important to consider the implications of such gender-related patterns of achievement.

Although girls are excelling in English, it is an English that focuses upon what has been described as nineteenth-century literary and literacy habits, rather than literacy in computer and communications media required in a rapidly changing world (Kress, 1998). Here we return to the issue of breadth of definitions of performance; but we should also consider the implications of gendered subject preferences. It is currently the subjects that are disproportionally taken by males at the higher levels, such as computer studies,

FIGURE 2.8 The relationship between educational attainment and work is not a straightforward one

engineering, and physical sciences, that are highly valued in our society, and that often reap the highest financial rewards in the world of work. Kress warns that, if we ignore the growing divide between the world of school and work, then 'Girls' achievement would be rewarded by the education system; but not by the world of work' (1998, p.5). Reflections such as these indicate that the uncertainties generated by shifts in performance patterns and employment opportunities do not have straightforward implications.

4.3 Gendered identities and school performance

In Section 4.3 we will look at the construction of a social science argument, using the example of educational achievement differences. As Patricia Murphy and Jannette Elwood (1998) suggest that typically masculine and typically feminine attributes are developed through interactions with parents, peers and schooling (and other such social agents) from infancy. They provide evidence suggesting that masculine and feminine attributes are differentially perceived and rewarded within the structures of our education system.

They front their research by arguing:

> The question considered in this paper is not what girls and boys can or cannot do; but what it is that girls and boys *choose* to do. What lies behind their choices and how do gendered choices influences achievement?

(Murphy and Elwood, 1998, p.95)

Notice Murphy and Elwood's focus on choices and influences on those choices. They suggest that certain factors impact on personal agency with regard to subject choice and achievement, and build up their argument by exploring a number of claims. We will use the evidence they have gathered to explore three claims that they believe provide an explanation of school performance in terms of gendered identity:

- *Claim 1:* 'Boys' and 'girls' foster different interests, attitudes, and behaviours prior to attending school, which are then perpetuated within school.

- *Claim 2:* Feminine and masculine identities are perceived in particular ways by teachers, with consequences that may impinge on achievement.

- *Claim 3:* In their school-work, 'girls' and 'boys' draw upon the different interests and skills that they have developed through their gendered experiences. However, the sorts of knowledge and style of expression produced by 'girls' and by 'boys' are often differentially rewarded. Typically masculine forms of expression are more highly rewarded in some subject areas (such as the sciences), and typically feminine forms of expression in others (such as English).

Murphy and Elwood (1998) use quotation marks around the words 'boys' and 'girls' when they want to denote reference to boys with typically masculine and girls with typically feminine interests, behaviour and traits. We have followed this convention when referring to their work.

The first claim suggests that children arrive at school with gendered interests and behaviours. On the basis of previous research, Murphy and Elwood propose that culturally-based socialization practices structure the experiences of 'girls' and 'boys', and can account for gendered identities.

Murphy and Elwood highlight how 'girls' and 'boys' develop interests in different types of play, with girls typically enjoying creative activities, and

FIGURE 2.9 Children first learn about gender-appropriate behaviour from their immediate world

boys typically enjoying constructional activities. In participating in different activities 'girls' and 'boys' consequently acquire different skills associated with those activities. Different interests are also developed with regard to discussion and reading topics that 'girls' and 'boys' enjoy and this contributes to the construction of masculine and feminine identities. Murphy and Elwood assert that, if children are familiar with the activities and topics they encounter at school, they will have confidence in pursuing them; but if the activities they encounter are at odds with their interests, they are likely to lack confidence and become alienated from their tasks. This leads 'boys' and 'girls' to make particular choices and engage with certain school activities and not with others. Murphy and Elwood (1998) focus on science classes as an example of this. 'Boys' have typically had more experience with scientific apparatus outside school contexts, and they adapt to the use of similar equipment within science lessons better than do 'girls'. 'Boys' maintain their advantage through dominating use of the equipment.

FIGURE 2.10   Do girls and boys have equal opportunities in practical science work?

Jackson (1998) also highlights how school knowledge, which as we have seen is narrowly defined, serves to engage some children and alienate others:

> This has undermined the abilities and destroyed the confidence and motivation of many working-class girls, members of ethnic and cultural minorities and some working-class boys. Many boys have felt brushed aside by the dominant definition of school knowledge – their home and community languages, their often raw but direct insights and their everyday, street knowledges have all been experienced as invalid.

(Jackson, 1998, p.79)

The second claim suggests that teachers react to gendered identities as expressed within school contexts in particular ways. Teacher interventions, non-interventions, and responses may well complement the choices that children are already making. Murphy and Elwood note how lack of confidence, typically experienced by girls in relation to certain topics, '... is all too often interpreted as lack of ability' (1998, p.102). Other characteristically masculine and feminine behaviours are also interpreted by teachers with subtle but important consequences. Thinking back to the study by Francis reported in Box 2.2, you will remember that in general girls' attitudes tend to be more conforming than those of boys in school contexts. Whilst this conformity may be highly regarded by teachers, in comparison to the risky, gambling approach that some boys take to their work, it can be taken as evidence of less (or, more usually, very 'average') ability. The more unusual, less conformist approach adopted by some boys is often taken as indication of an acute brain, a 'bright spark'. Similar expectations have been found in children's and young people's self-perceptions, with boys typically overrating their abilities, whilst girls underrate theirs (Joffe and Foxman, 1988).

Murphy and Elwood suggest that the judgements that teachers make of ability can have direct implications for performance. One example provided is that, in 1994, 5 per cent more females than males were entered for the middle band of the GCSE mathematics exam (in which a C grade is the highest level awarded). More boys were entered for the higher band (which risks an unclassified grading if performance drops below grade C). Murphy and Elwood point out that this may be a consequence of teachers' *perceptions* of females' confidence in mathematics, and *judgements* made about their anxiety.

The third claim argues that particular styles, expressions, and representations of knowledge are valued in particular subjects areas, and that these correspond to masculine and feminine favoured work styles. In other words, performance is dependent upon the style of response presented, and this differentially affects 'girls' and 'boys' depending upon the subject matter.

ACTIVITY 2.4

Figures 2.11 and 2.12, reproduced from Murphy and Elwood (1998), are typical examples of drawings which children produced when asked to design a boat to go around the world, giving details of things that were important.

Look at these pictures in some detail. What differences do you see between the girl's picture and the boy's picture?

FIGURE 2.11

A typical girl's boat

Source: Murphy and Elwood, 1998, p.104

FIGURE 2.12

A typical boy's boat

Source: Murphy and Elwood, 1998, p.104

COMMENT

We noticed that the girl's picture in Figure 2.11 features details of the furniture and home comforts that she considers important for a trip around the world. In contrast, the boy's picture in Figure 2.12 concentrates on the design of the boat. It appears as if the children interpreted the question in very different ways. The girl attended to the details for the people who would be living on the boat, and the boy attended to the construction of the boat itself that would enable it to get around the world. The concern that 'girls' hold about human needs are typically at odds with the more context-free requirements of school science. In this scenario, if the teacher had intended the construction of the boat to be the focus of the task, then this effectively undervalues 'girls'' perceptions of the task, and generally 'boys'' work would gain higher marks.

We have already noted how the literacy styles and interests of boys and girls differ before and during, as well as outside and inside, school. The argument is made by Murphy and Elwood that the different interests, activities, and experiences of 'boys' and 'girls' affect the work done in school and lead to differences in examination performance. Although 'boys' may be very good at dealing with presenting facts, this is not what is required in English exams and they consequently tend to underachieve in this area. In contrast, 'boys'' analytical styles are rewarded within science, whereas 'girls' may not have had the experience to develop appropriate expression in this area. The work of Murphy and Elwood suggests that examination results reflect gendered identities, rather than a divergence in ability levels between 'boys' and 'girls'.

At the end of their paper, Murphy and Elwood comment on the importance of considering socio-economic backgrounds in relation to achievement. This is a crucial issue. Furthermore, not all boys are failing, and not all girls are out-achieving boys. Identity and academic achievement is not just an issue of gender; it also embodies issues of individual differences, social and economic groupings, ethnicity, and nationality.

SUMMARY

- At the end of the twentieth and the beginning of the twenty-first centuries there has been much media interest in the 'crisis' of boys' underachievement. Generally, boys do seem to be doing less well than girls in GCSEs; but the picture is more complex as it relates to particular groups of boys and girls, and involves many other influences, such as class and ethnicity.

- Results of cognitive testing indicate that men and women have strengths in different sorts of tasks. Although this is suggestive of *natural* innate differences, evidence suggests that social and cultural factors may account for some of the results.

- There are concerns about the validity of school examinations. School knowledge is narrowly defined and this alienates particular groups of children.

- Particular school subjects and examinations, as currently defined, may reward the ways of working and styles of expression typically adopted by girls, whilst other subjects may reward boys' typical work styles.

- There are individual differences in relation to school performance, as well as diversity between groups of boys and girls. This is partly related to the multidimensionality of identity, and the range of masculinities and femininities existing in our social world.

- Consideration of the implications of gender differences in schooling suggests that there may potentially be continuities in trends (such as the low status of 'women's work') despite important recent changes.

5 CONCLUSION

In this chapter we have investigated gender identities through looking at gender categories – how we construct and use them, and how we come to consider ourselves as gendered beings. We have found that gendered identities have repercussions for experiences at school, educational performance, and economic life chances.

We started this chapter with two claims. The first was that gender identities are shaped by many different factors. We found that biological factors (such as the forms of our bodies, or the genetic material inside them) and social factors (such as the experiences we have inside and outside schools) are not independent. Gender identity, like identity more generally, is a complex interweaving of a variety of different influences: biological factors that are affected by the environment (for example through our cultural perceptions of biology), and social factors that are influenced through our (often rather naïve) understandings of biology. Secondly, we claimed that the way we construct our identities is strongly influenced by feminine and masculine characteristics associated with the gender categories, men and women. We have seen evidence that as individuals we can choose which aspects of gender identity to take up, but our choices are constrained by a variety of factors, including cultural perceptions of masculinity and femininity.

To explore the flexibility of gender categories and the diversity of gender identities we have looked at development from childhood to adulthood, and seen how developing an understanding of gender involves a search for certainty. In early childhood, gender categories are used in a fixed, often stereotypical, essentialist way, but gradually, as children learn more about their social world, gender categories become more sophisticated and flexible. This increasing flexibility accommodates a diversity of masculinities and femininities. It is clear that gender identities are not fixed; they shift and change across time and between cultures. However, evidence suggests that our identities are not something that we are completely free to choose and use exactly as we want; they are shaped by society, the culture that we live in, and our experiences and understandings. The identities of particular groups of males and females may be constrained or liberated when pitched against historical agendas and social structures, such as education and the economy. Although we may feel free to choose our identities, social and cultural factors, which include class and ethnicity as well as gender, contribute to the sorts of identities that we hold.

Murphy and Elwood's argument was studied in some detail because they made an explicit explanatory claim linking gender identities to the gendered achievement patterns seen in examination results. Their evidence suggests that particular sorts of knowledge and styles of expression are required by different school subjects, and that these subject-specific requirements differentially benefit 'boys' and 'girls'. Murphy and Elwood suggest that if school children were more aware of the different styles of expression expected in different subject areas, and were taught skills to deal with these requirements, then perhaps gendered inequalities in achievement patterns would diminish. The evidence they present is powerfully illustrative of the gradual process of identity formation and the consequences of living with gendered identities.

REFERENCES

Bem, S.L. (1974) 'The measurement of psychological androgyny', *Journal of Consulting and Clinical Psychology,* vol.42, pp.155–62.

Bem, S.L. (1989) 'Genital knowledge and gender constancy in pre-school children', *Child Development*, vol.60, pp.649–62.

Birke, L. (1992) 'In pursuit of difference: scientific studies of women and men' in Kirkup, G. and Keller, L.S (eds) *Inventing Women: Science, Technology and Gender*, Cambridge, Polity.

Connell, R.W. (1987) *Gender and Power: Society, the Person, and Sexual Politics*, Oxford, Basil Blackwell.

Durkin, K. (1995) *Developmental Social Psychology, from Infancy to Old Age*, Oxford, Blackwell.

Elton, B. and Curtis, R. (1998) *Blackadder II: Bells* in Curtis, R., Elton, B. Lloyd, J. and Atkinson, R. *BlackAdder: The Whole Damn Dynasty*, London, Michael Joseph.

Francis, B. (1997) 'Power plays: children's constructions of gender and power in role plays', *Gender and Education*, vol.9, pp.179–91.

Francis, B. (1998) 'Oppositional positions: children's construction of gender in talk and role plays based on adult occupation', *Educational Research*, vol. 40, no.1, pp.31–43.

Jackson, D. (1998) 'Breaking out of the binary trap: boys' underachievement, schooling and gender relations' in Epstein, D., Elwood, J., Hey, V. and Maw, J. (eds) *Failing Boys? Issues in Gender and Achievement*, Buckingham, Open University Press.

Joffe, L. and Foxman, D. (1988) *Attitudes and Gender Differences*, Slough, NFER/Nelson.

Kimura, D. (1992) 'Sex differences in the brain', *Scientific American*, September, pp.81–7.

Kohlberg, L. (1966) 'A cognitive-developmental analysis of children's sex-role concepts and attitudes' in Maccoby, E.E. (ed.) *The Development of Sex Differences,* Stanford, CA, Stanford University Press.

Kress, G. (1998) 'The future still belongs to boys', *The Independent (Education),* 11 June, pp.4–5.

Mac an Ghaill, M. (1994) *The Making of Men: Masculinities, Sexualities and Schooling,* Buckingham, Open University Press.

Murphy, P. and Elwood, J. (1998) 'Gendered experiences, choices and achievements – exploring the links', *Journal of Inclusive Education,* vol.2, no.2, pp.95–118.

Paechter, C. (1998) *Educating the Other: Gender, Power and Schooling,* London, The Falmer Press.

Summerfield, P. (1987) 'Cultural reproduction in the education of girls: a study of girls' secondary schooling in two Lancashire towns 1900–50' in Hunt, F. (ed.) *Lessons for Life,* Oxford, Basil Blackwell.

Turner, J.C., Hogg, M.A., Oakes, P.J., Reicher, S.D. and Wetherell, M. (1987) *Rediscovering the Social Group: A Self-Categorization Theory,* Oxford, Basil Blackwell.

Turner, P.J. (1995) *Sex, Gender and Identity,* Leicester, The British Psychological Society.

FURTHER READING

Sandra Lipsitz Bem (1993) *The Lenses of Gender: Transforming the Debate on Sexual Inequality,* London, Yale University Press. This book argues that, to achieve true gender equality, we need to study the hidden assumptions about sex and gender that pervade our society and culture. Bem's thought-provoking book tries to reveal and then dismantle these assumptions, arguing that society need not – and should not – be organized around the difference between men and women.

Vivien Burr (1998) *Gender and Social Psychology,* London, Routledge. This book gives a clear introduction to the psychology of gender, without assuming a detailed knowledge of psychology. Burr looks at gender differences in a variety of arenas – education, work, and the media – and at some methods used to study gender.

Identity, inequality and social class

Maureen Mackintosh and Gerry Mooney

Contents

1 INTRODUCTION: WORK, INCOMES AND IDENTITY

In Chapter 1, Kath Woodward pointed out how often we ask, 'What is it that you do?' when we meet someone for the first time. This question is not only a means of establishing contact, it also mirrors understandings about how we see ourselves and our world, and how we see others. It presumes a relationship between a person's occupation and his or her identity.

It tends to be paid work that is emphasized in these conversations. Housework or unpaid caring for relatives and family members seem only to define us – as 'carers' or 'housewives' – when we do not also do paid work. This is partly because paid work brings us money to live on. Paid work is also a source of collective identity through relationships with colleagues at work.

In this chapter we examine how income and paid work are closely related sources of individual and collective identity. The pattern of employment and the distribution of incomes are both important structures that shape our identity, as is the way we spend our incomes (our lifestyle). However, there is no simple causal link between what we have and do, and who we are. This is not only because there are other sources of identity besides work and income (as Chapters 1 and 2 showed), it is also because the link between these economic structures and identity is mediated by *representation* (a concept introduced in Chapter 1). How we feel about our job (or lack of one) and our income depends on what others have and how others see us.

Such representations include, for example, classifying some people as 'poor', others as 'working class', yet others as 'middle class'. People may adopt these representations of themselves or they may contest them. One important way in which occupation is linked to identity is thus through the deeply contested notion of social class. The UK is often seen as a class-ridden society. In Chapter 1 for example, an ex-coalminer described the devastation that the wave of closures of mines and heavy industries in the 1980s brought to the identities of people in one working community. In the wake of these kinds of occupational changes, the government announced in 1998 a new social classification of the population, rewritten in terms of newly dominant job categories such as service jobs. Figure 3.1 shows the new classifications and some of the occupations associated with them.

The papers were quick to headline the new social classification 'We're all middle class now'.

The chapter looks at how identities are represented and shaped within economic structures. Section 2 shows how poverty is represented and how being poor shapes identities. Sections 3 and 4 examine some economic

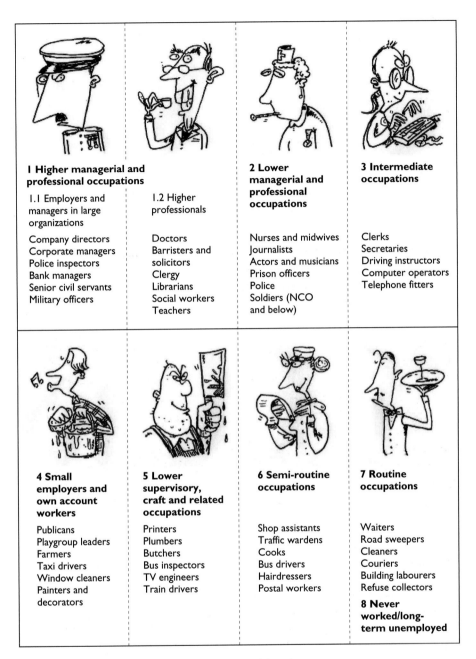

1 Higher managerial and professional occupations

1.1 Employers and managers in large organizations

Company directors
Corporate managers
Police inspectors
Bank managers
Senior civil servants
Military officers

1.2 Higher professionals

Doctors
Barristers and solicitors
Clergy
Librarians
Social workers
Teachers

2 Lower managerial and professional occupations

Nurses and midwives
Journalists
Actors and musicians
Prison officers
Police
Soldiers (NCO and below)

3 Intermediate occupations

Clerks
Secretaries
Driving instructors
Computer operators
Telephone fitters

4 Small employers and own account workers

Publicans
Playgroup leaders
Farmers
Taxi drivers
Window cleaners
Painters and decorators

5 Lower supervisory, craft and related occupations

Printers
Plumbers
Butchers
Bus inspectors
TV engineers
Train drivers

6 Semi-routine occupations

Shop assistants
Traffic wardens
Cooks
Bus drivers
Hairdressers
Postal workers

7 Routine occupations

Waiters
Road sweepers
Cleaners
Couriers
Building labourers
Refuse collectors

8 Never worked/long-term unemployed

FIGURE 3.1   Where you rate in the new social order

Source: *The Guardian*, 15 January 1999, p.3

structures and focus on inequality, wealth, power and class. Section 5 explores some explanations of social class and Section 6 shifts the emphasis onto consumption as a source of identity. Section 7 revisits the different interpretations of inequality and explores change and uncertainty in the contemporary UK, in the context of social exclusion.

2 WHAT IT IS TO BE POOR

When you say that someone is 'poor', what do you mean?

Do people whom others call 'poor' always see themselves in that way?

One group whose identities are greatly constrained by income are the poor. But, as the questions above suggest, poverty is not a simple fact of some lives: rather, it is a concept with different meanings, and a label that we may accept or reject. This section considers how poverty shapes identity.

2.1 'Making ends meet'

When people talk about being poor, they often talk about the difficulty of being able to 'make ends meet' on low incomes. The phrase evokes people's experience of the daily struggle to feed and clothe a family on very little money, to keep them warm, dry, clean and safe, and to do this without getting into debt or getting into trouble. Some low income families in the UK live on social security benefits alone and have very little other access to cash or formal sources of credit. The result is a very basic existence:

> I don't smoke, I don't drink, I don't go out, I don't eat meat. I have thought of getting rid of the TV but I can't because it's for [my son] ... I think, 'Shall I get rid of the cat?' but I can't ... There's absolutely nothing I spend money on except just surviving, you know, paying bills and buying food.
>
> (quoted in Kempson, 1996, p.49)

This quotation is drawn from a survey of life on low incomes in the early to mid 1990s (Kempson, 1996). The survey was based on 31 studies that had been funded by the Joseph Rowntree Foundation. The people interviewed in the studies were diverse in terms of age, ethnicity, geographical location and life experience. Kempson's survey concluded that people who had been 'on benefits' for a while generally faced a hard choice between going without essentials or falling behind with their bills for water, electricity, gas or rent. The longer people live on low incomes, the harder it gets to cope. Children grow, clothes wear out, appliances need replacing, school activities cost money, isolation gets worse because of lack of money to socialize, and health and mental energy are undermined. Kempson concluded that UK benefit rates in the early 1990s generally gave people insufficient money to cover even basic needs. As one benefit recipient said: 'You're on the poverty line whichever way you look at it ... Nobody can manage on £46 a week. You can't exist on that. You can't manage it. It's degrading' (quoted in Kempson, 1996, p.6).

Many low income households in the UK, however, do not claim state benefits. Many people live on low wages, and the extent of very low paid work increased in the 1980s and 1990s. In the Rowntree studies reported in Kempson, wages of £70–£90 a week for such full time jobs as shop assistant, and around £100 for male manual jobs, were quite commonly reported.

So how much is enough to 'make ends meet'? The Rowntree studies asked this question in a variety of ways. The people interviewed were asked how much money they needed to cover basic outgoings, to live on, to avoid the need to supplement low wages, to create a low likelihood of problem debt. The different calculations produced some remarkably similar answers despite the diversity of people interviewed. Single people reckoned that in the early 1990s they needed about £150 a week, or less if they were not a householder. Lone parents came up with a figure of around £180 a week. Couples with children needed around £200 to avoid arrears on bills. Many people on low wages were working long hours to try to bring their incomes up to these figures (Kempson, 1996).

The consistency of these estimates suggests that, in a particular time and place, there tends to be a shared view about what goods and services are necessities. The UK government also takes a view on this issue. It states that the level of Income Support – the basic benefit for adults – should be 'the amount needed to bring their income up to their "applicable amount". This is the level the law says they need to live on' (DSS, 1997, p.21). Income Support payments vary according to family circumstances and housing costs. The number of people living at or below the Income Support 'poverty line' is frequently used as one definition of those counted as 'poor' in the UK. The Rowntree studies showed that by the early 1990s these benefit payments had fallen below a social consensus on the level that was necessary.

FIGURE 3.2 Urban poverty – Possil Park, Glasgow. In 1998, Possil Park was named the most deprived area in Scotland

2.2 Necessities and luxuries

As the division of opinion between the government and low income people illustrates, definitions of poverty are the stuff of political debate. People in the Rowntree studies tended to focus on 'paying bills and food'. Most people's list of basic needs would also include adequate food and clean water, clothing, shelter and heating. But are there also less apparently physiological, more evidently social, necessities of life?

ACTIVITY 3.1

Look back at the quotation early in this section. A woman on a low income seems to be arguing that a TV is a 'necessity' for her son.

What do you think of her argument? Do you think a TV a 'luxury' or a 'necessity' in the contemporary UK?

Decide what you think and why before reading on.

COMMENT

Televisions were not a necessity in the 1930s since they were not available. But how about in the UK today? You may have answered, no, a TV cannot be a 'necessity' because one can stay alive without a TV. But what about living a human life, with enough sociability and communication to make life worthwhile? Many accounts of the experience of poverty include the pain of social isolation: of not being able to afford to socialize with your peers. Communication with others is part of being human, and in a society where virtually everyone has access to a TV at home, people without television are deprived of access to one of the staples of conversation, jokes and information exchange. Children can suffer particularly from limited access to a shared culture – something the mother quoted above was trying to avoid for her son.

So one might conclude that in the UK, where 96 per cent of households had a television in 1994, it is now a 'necessity'. A lack of a TV constitutes relative deprivation if all the other children in the class have access to one *and* it has become a basic means of communication and cultural reference point. By the same token we could argue that a radio was a necessity in Britain in the 1940s. A TV seems to be a necessity at the end of the twentieth century; a computer may become a necessity in future years if using one becomes a common way to bank, shop and communicate.

There is no 'right answer' to Activity 3.1. Necessities are a matter of social and political judgement. But that does not mean our definitions are arbitrary. In 1990 a study called *Breadline Britain* asked 1800 people whether a number of items were 'necessities'; 58 per cent put a TV in that category, up from 51 per cent in a similar survey in 1983 (Goodman *et al.*, 1997, p.244). Our ideas about what we need depend on what others have and what others expect. Even notions of what constitutes adequate food and heating have changed over time. Social scientists therefore generally recognize that there is a strong 'relative' element in definitions of **poverty**. That is, there are some irreducible human needs, but poverty in a society is also defined relative to the goods, services and opportunities available to the non-poor.

Poverty
Poverty is more than a lack of money. It carries a stigma because it is defined relative to what people think is needed for a decent life.

2.3 How others see us

The relative nature of poverty is an old theme in social science. Adam Smith, the eighteenth century writer who is often regarded as the founding father of economics, put it this way: 'By necessaries I understand not only the commodities that are indispensably necessary for the support of life, but whatever the custom of the country renders it indecent for creditable people, even the lowest orders, to be without' (Smith, 1776, quoted in Sen, 1981).

Ideas of what it is to be poor are thus closely tied up with difficulty in maintaining the basic decencies of life. In the Rowntree studies, people on low incomes repeatedly referred to fear, for example fear of homelessness or disconnection from water, heat and power; to shame, especially shame at getting into debt; and to guilt about having to ask others for help. 'When they turned the water tap off, I felt very upset, I can't explain ... I feel personally ashamed. I feel ashamed at myself' (quoted in Kempson, 1996, p.37).

As a result, the idea of being 'poor' carries a **stigma**: it is a label that many people living on low incomes resist. For example, in a set of interviews in the early 1990s, 85 social security claimants were asked whether they thought 'poverty' existed in Britain, and if so, who were the poor and were they themselves 'poor'? Almost everyone could answer these questions, and almost two thirds of interviewees said that they did not consider themselves to be poor. Half of the rest admitted reluctance in defining themselves as poor. The answers were also gendered. Men were more likely than women to deny poverty, suggesting that men may be more likely to be ashamed and women more realistic, as this short extract from an interview shows:

Stigma
An attribute that is perceived by others as demeaning or discrediting for those who have it. It can be social or physical or a characteristic shared by a whole group or by a few individuals. Stigma is used to justify exclusion.

Interviewer Do you think poverty still exists in this country?

Respondent (man) It don't.

Respondent's wife It does!

Respondent We're not poverty-stricken, nowhere near it yet. We've got all the stuff we can sell.

Respondent's wife But that doesn't mean we've got food in the cupboard ...

(quoted in Dean, 1992, p.83)

The interviewees in the survey expressed many different meanings of the word poverty. Some saw poverty more as a state of mind than a fact: poor people were 'people who think they're poor', an idea often associated with the notion that people bring poverty upon themselves. The survey author comments that some interviewees seemed to see the admission of poverty as a kind of self-indulgence: they insisted that there were many worse off than themselves, or that 'real' poverty no longer existed. Others felt that poverty implied a lack of dignity or cleanliness and cited their clean homes as evidence that they were not poor. Others straightforwardly resisted what they saw as an undesirable classification: some said that they did not 'class' themselves as 'poor', but as 'ordinary working class'.

Poverty is therefore not only a relative matter. Representations of the poor in British culture are often demeaning. As a result of these derogatory meanings, it is hard for people struggling on low incomes to identify themselves as 'poor' and to use that identity in campaigning at the level of national policy. National anti-poverty lobbying has been largely conducted by 'experts' and professional campaign groups. This is in contrast to the effective organization and national lobbying carried out on their own behalf by, for example, people with disabilities (many of whom suffer from poverty) who have fought to change public representations of disability and to change social and individual expectations (Beresford and Croft, 1995). Campaigns of this kind require people to identify with a label; but, as a participant in one conference that brought together anti-poverty campaigners and people with experience of poverty put it: 'I think this word poverty is a real crusher' (Lister and Beresford, 1991, p.10).

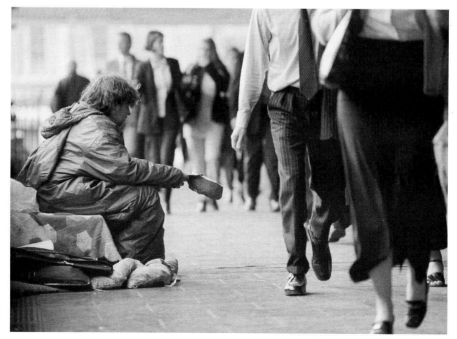

FIGURE 3.3
A homeless man begging from commuters

SUMMARY

- Claims about who is *poor* are rooted in shared and contested ideas about the basic necessities of life.
- The experience of *poverty* is both *relative* and *relational*. It is defined by what people have, and what they can do, relative to the opportunities of others.
- *Poverty* carries derogatory meanings, so it does not easily provide a basis for collective identity.

3 WORK, INCOMES AND INEQUALITY

It is not only poverty that is relative and relational: throughout the income scale people define and experience their economic position through ideas about the incomes and opportunities of others. Our identities are, therefore, influenced by the shape of the income distribution. What we mean by this phrase is that it matters to our sense of ourselves whether we imagine that most people's incomes are 'in the middle' or whether we see incomes as polarized between rich and poor. This section takes a look at what the data show.

3.1 Describing inequality

One of the most graphic ways of describing the distribution of incomes is by using the 'income parade' that was invented by a Dutch economist, Jan Pen. It conjures up, in the words of two British economists who have lined up a new UK parade, 'a surreal world where the height of each person in the UK had been stretched in proportion to his or her income, and then everyone was lined up in order of height, the shortest (poorest) on the left and the tallest (richest) on the right' (Jenkins and Cowell, 1994).

Pen imagined his parade passing by in one hour, and talked the reader through the experience. The same can be done using UK data on incomes for the early 1990s, with 56 million people in the line-up. People zip along in the parade with the other members of their household. (All the detail of the UK parade given in this chapter is drawn from Hills, 1995, vol.2.)

The average height in our UK parade is 5ft 8in: that is the height given to each of a couple with average household income. (As the heights given in the Hills report are in feet and inches, we have decided to use these rather than changing them to metric values.) The incomes used in constructing the parade are *household* incomes (otherwise a non-earning partner of an earner

ave income
Nº of household

would appear – wrongly – as destitute). And the incomes are adjusted – in ways that are described briefly below – for the costs of supporting children and for the numbers of adults in the household. So by 'average' household income we mean the total of these adjusted household incomes divided by the number of households.

So how does the parade look? Bizarre, really. Almost everyone is tiny relative to the few 'giants' who arrive at the end of the parade. After three minutes a single unemployed mother with two small children, living below the Income Support level, goes past: she is about 1ft 10in high. Six minutes later a single male pensioner, owning his own home and claiming Income Support, passes by: he is about 2ft 6in high. Everyone in the first 12 minutes has less than half average incomes, so is below 2ft 10in high. After 21 minutes a childless couple go by: he is a full time vehicle exhaust fitter, she does not do paid work; they are both 3ft 9in high.

You might expect that as the half hour strikes, the people going past will be of average height (that is, average income). But far from being 5ft 8in high, the person who passes you after 30 minutes is only 4ft 10in high, with a household income only 83 per cent of the average. We don't see the household with average income until 62 per cent of the population have passed us. After about 45 minutes, a couple go by with a baby and a toddler: the man is a full time technician in an engineering firm, and the woman works part time as a telephonist. They are both 6ft 10in high.

It is only at ten minutes to the hour that heights really start to grow. With nine minutes to go, a single woman aged 45 without children comes by. She is a full time personnel officer and 8ft 7in high. With three minutes left, a couple in their late fifties whose children have left home pass by. He is a self-employed freelance journalist and she is a part-time manager of a day centre for the elderly. They are both 11ft 11in high. And still the real giants have not arrived. In the last minute a company chief executive and his non-earning wife pass by: they are both at least 60ft high. And in the very last seconds of the parade, the scene changes dramatically. As Pen described those seconds, 'suddenly: the scene is dominated by colossal figures: people like tower flats ... the rear of the parade is brought up by a few participants who are measured in miles ... their heads disappear into the clouds.' (cited in Hills, 1995, vol.2). A modest estimate of the income of Britain's richest man would make him and his partner each four miles high.

This extraordinarily graphic image of income distribution is also very exact. By lining up households in order of income it allows us to compare household incomes, and, as we will now show, to measure changes in inequality over time. Let us look at the parade a little more carefully. Remember, people are classified by household income and that income has been adjusted to allow for the number of people in the household and their ages. The idea is quite simple (though the calculations are not!). Income is based on a couple without children. A single person with an income that is the same as a couple's income will have that income adjusted upwards –

since only one person lives on it, it represents a higher level of income for that one person than for a couple. A couple with children would have the same income adjusted downwards: more people live on it so there is less for each. The resultant 'equivalent' income is what is measured to allocate places in the parade. (Hills, 1995, vol.2; DSS, 1997).

Finally, let's look at those 'averages'. One of the things the income parade shows is that 62 per cent of the UK population lives on less than average income. How can this be? Why is it not 50 per cent? Why *didn't* the 5ft 8in high person zip by on the half hour? The answer lies in the structure of the parade. There are many more poor people than rich, but the top incomes, though very few, are *very* large. So the average (calculated by dividing the total household income by the number of households) is influenced strongly by that couple who are four miles high. The four-mile-highers pull up the average, so the person half-way along the parade has much less than average income.

Suppose we take our UK parade and put in a marker every six minutes. We have then divided our parade into tenths, with the poorest tenth on the left and the richest tenth on the right. We can then pick out the (adjusted) household incomes for the household halfway along each tenth. This gives a picture like that shown in Figure 3.4, which is one representation of the shape of the UK income distribution in the mid 1990s.

FIGURE 3.4   Tenths of the income distribution, from poor to rich: income of the middle household in each tenth

Source: based on data from DSS, 1997, Table A2

Look carefully at Figure 3.4. Looking along the bottom, you can see that each bar represents a tenth of the population, with the poorest tenth at the left, just as in the income parade. The height of the bar represents the adjusted household income for the household half-way along each tenth. The income is measured up the vertical axis in £s. If you look at Figure 3.4. you will see that there is no scale on the vertical axis, this is because we want you to examine your own perceptions of the UK income distribution.

Think back to the mid 1990s. To get into the *top tenth* of the income distribution, that is, to be better off than 90 per cent of the UK population, how much do you think a single person would have needed to earn? How about a childless couple or a couple with two children? Remember that a single person needs less for the same standard of living than a couple with children. If you get a chance, ask a few other people their opinions.

Try to guess before you look at the answer given at the end of the chapter: this activity is about perceptions of inequality, not a test of general knowledge!

COMMENT

How did you get on? Guesses vary of course, but it is common for people to overestimate what you need to earn to live better than 90 per cent of the population. Politicians make this kind of mistake all the time. They have been known to refer to £30,000 a year as 'middle income', whereas those earnings would take even a couple with children into the top 30 per cent of the income distribution. It is also common to underestimate just how much difference children make, that is, how expensive they really are! The person half-way along the parade described above is one of a childless couple with one person earning a little more than £16,000 a year (Goodman *et al.*, 1997).

This activity also illustrates how socially and economically varied the top tenth is. A single person earning £22,000 has little in common with the merchant bankers and business directors at the very end of the parade. The income differences within the top tenth are *far* larger than elsewhere: that was one point of the parade.

3.2 Increasing inequality

Inequality in incomes got worse during the 1980s and early 1990s. Dividing the income parade into tenths offers us a neat way of displaying this increasing inequality. Look first at Figure 3.5. Each of the vertical bars shows the percentage change in income between 1961 and 1979 for the person who occurs mid-way along each of the tenths of the population, lined up as in our parade. The higher the bar, the higher the percentage change. So the poorest tenth of the population had an increase in income of over 50 per cent. (These are 'real' incomes; that is, adjusted to take out the effects of general price inflation and to estimate what the incomes will buy.) The other tenths had an increase of about one third. So overall, the people at the beginning of the parade got a *little* larger (but only by a very small amount) relative to the people coming by later on (Hills, 1996).

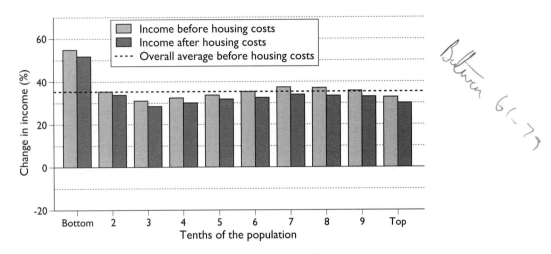

FIGURE 3.5 Change in real after-tax income, by tenths of the population, 1961–79
Source: Hills, 1996, p.4

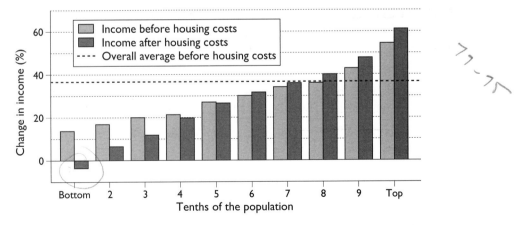

FIGURE 3.6 Change in real after-tax income, by tenths of the population, 1979–1994/5
Source: DSS, 1997, p.69

Between 1979 and 1994–5, within the years of Conservative government, a quite different pattern emerges. The contrast is genuinely startling. In those years, as Figure 3.6 shows, the increases in income were concentrated in the better-off tenths of the population. The pattern is consistent. The richest tenth got the largest percentage increase, then the next, and so on down to the poorest. Furthermore, if the incomes are calculated after people have paid for housing – an essential expenditure with costs that vary hugely across the country – then those people earliest in the parade actually shrank: the poorest tenth of the population saw their income fall. Income distribution in the years shown in Figure 3.6 became much more unequal (DSS, 1997; Hills, 1996).

So in the 1980s and early 1990s the gap between poor and rich widened dramatically. There was a significant rise in the numbers in poverty, as measured by income. A common measure of numbers in poverty is those who are living in households at or below half of average (adjusted) incomes. In our early 1990s parade, everyone in the first two tenths fell into this group. Between 1979 and 1991–2 the number of people living in households at or below half of average incomes (after housing costs) rose from 5.0 million to 13.9 million. Of those 13.9 million, 6.0 million had incomes below half the *1979* average (Hills, 1995, p.32).

Given the number of people involved, 'the poor' are, of course, very diverse. If you are a single parent (most of whom are female) or unemployed then you are very likely to find yourself in this group. A third of single pensioners and 27 per cent of households supported by part time workers are there too. The risk of poverty is high for the long-term sick and for people with disabilities. Members of some ethnic minorities are also much more likely than the white population to find themselves in the bottom fifth of the income distribution (Goodman *et al.*, 1997). This diversity shows how being 'poor' interacts with other sources of identity, such as gender and ethnicity.

SUMMARY

- The UK income distribution is highly unequal, and has been becoming more so.
- Well over half the UK population live below average incomes.
- A few wealthy people have extraordinarily high incomes relative to everyone else.
- The numbers in poverty rose sharply in the 1980s and early 1990s.
- Important determinants of where you are in the income distribution are occupation and household structure, including the number of children within the household.

4 WEALTH, POWER AND CLASS

The further you are down the income distribution, the more you are likely to experience income as a structural constraint. The wealthier you are, conversely, the more you may be aware of income and wealth as sources of opportunity and of power over others.

4.1 Wealth and class identity

Income is very unequal in the UK, but wealth holding is even more dramatically unequal. Data on the very wealthy are hard to collect, but according to the Inland Revenue (the only collectors of non-voluntary data!) in 2000 over half (53 per cent) the **financial wealth** in the UK was owned by 10 per cent of the population (Inland Revenue in *Social Trends*, 2002). Conversely, most people have virtually no financial cushion. The less wealthy half of the UK population in the 1990s had less than £500 per household in savings (and owned only 6 per cent in total of the financial wealth), while the least wealthy quarter had savings of less than £50 (Banks *et al.*, 1996; Hills, 1995; ONS, 1998).

Financial wealth
This includes savings, company shares, interest-earning loans and insurance policies.

Wealth and privilege are not very visible. The wealthy can withdraw into a private world of fee-paying schooling, private transport and health care, and social networks that are largely invisible to the non-wealthy. People in Britain, when asked to identify the privileged, tend to refer to an aristocracy or landed

FIGURE 3.7 Wealthy picnickers at Henley Royal Regatta: such images figure prominently in representations of the UK's 'upper class'

class, rather than their own managers and employers (Scott, 1994). This 'them and us', 'rich and poor' notion of social class is weakening but it is still influential and is fed by media images of the 'upper class' whose relationships and activities are represented in the popular media as being of enormous interest.

The weakening of these particular class distinctions is, in part, due to the spreading of private non-financial wealth downwards in the UK in the last 50 years. Houses and pension funds are also a form of wealth: 66 per cent of homes are now privately owned; 75 per cent of men working full time and 65 per cent of women working full time have occupational or individual private pensions. This is not 'wealth' in quite the same sense as financial assets: since we need them to live in and on, we cannot sell our houses and pensions without replacing them in some form. However, these forms of private wealth underpin 'middle class' living standards and self-perceptions. Adding them to financial wealth makes wealth distribution less unequal but even so the less wealthy half of the population still only own 10 per cent of the UK's wealth between them.

4.2 Wealth, capital and power

Wealth – even very modest wealth – brings some security and control. But among the wealthy, financial wealth and power are associated in a different way: wealth confers power over the lives of others. The very rich in the UK are either landowners, with inherited fortunes in landed property (particularly in urban areas), or they own fortunes derived from – and held in part as – shares in – manufacturing and service industries. Some of the richest landowners are from the old peerage: for example the Duke of Westminster's family estate includes much of Mayfair and Belgravia. Those holding fortunes in industry, commerce and finance are more diverse in origin. They include the inheritors of family industrial fortunes, such as the Sainsbury and the Pearson families. They also include first generation entrepreneurial wealth. The music business and computing have been routes for such self-made fortunes including, for example, those made by Alan Sugar who built up Amstrad, and Richard Branson of Virgin who started from a well-off professional background and made his first million selling hit records (Brown, 1988; Scott, 1994).

Most of the very wealthy are employers, either indirectly, through owning large shareholdings in companies, or as company directors. While the rest of us – if we own anything – usually have wealth in the form of houses and pensions, the top 1 per cent (those with wealth over £500,000 in 1994) held around 40 per cent of their wealth in company shares (Hills, 1995, p.98). A group of those with high incomes and wealth also work at managing the financial assets of others. Consider pension funds for example. You may have an occupational or private pension. If you do, the money you put into it each year will be managed on your behalf – and generally without your participation – by pension fund managers. They invest the funds: they lend them to governments and large companies, they buy commercial property to rent out and they buy company shares. Economists call finance used in this way 'capital'. It operates as the key link between wealth and power.

Wealthy business people thus invest their own capital and – predominantly – the capital of others in equipping businesses, in employing people and in producing goods and services. They respond to market opportunities in ways that shape our working lives. This economic system – the one within which most people in the world now live – is called **capitalism**.

Although historically relatively recent (barely two centuries old), capitalism has driven vast economic and social transformations. There has been a huge rise in total output of goods and services and enormous changes in the way we work and live, including huge international as well as national divergences in living standards. The perceived division capitalism has generated between those who own and manage capital and those who are employed is another enduring element of our notions of social class.

Capitalism
A system driven by the investment of private capital in large-scale production activities in pursuit of private profit.

SUMMARY

- Financial wealth is concentrated in few hands.
- Housing and pension wealth is somewhat more dispersed.
- Management of financial wealth as capital confers power.
- Both wealth, and power as an employer, are sources of class distinction.

5 SOCIAL CLASS

5.1 Seeing ourselves in class terms

Section 4 introduced two key elements of popular notions of social class: class as hierarchy, where those at the top do best, and class as oppositional, between those who own capital and those they employ. The *British Social Attitudes Survey* provides one regular source of evidence of how class permeates people's understanding of society. The 1995–96 edition showed that 69 per cent of people surveyed thought that a person's social class affected his or her opportunities a 'great deal' or 'quite a lot' (Jowell *et al.*, 1995). In a different 1996 survey, two-thirds of those interviewed agreed that 'there is one law for the rich and one law for the poor' and that 'ordinary people do not get their fair share of the nation's wealth' (Adonis and Pollard, 1998, p.11).

Social class can provide us with a sense of belonging; it can tell us who 'we' are and who 'they' are and, hence, how to relate to the world around us. Many people see the UK as a society sharply divided by class divisions and inequalities, but it does not follow that individuals have a strongly developed sense of class identity. Whether, or how strongly, you identify yourself as a member of a social class will be shaped by your personal history, including your family background, your occupation and your personal experiences of struggle and conflict. While some people, such as the interviewee quoted in Section 2, see 'working class' as a positive label they can identify with, others reject the term as stigmatizing or patronizing.

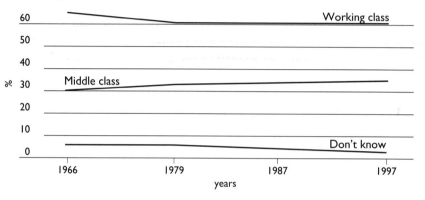

FIGURE 3.8 Most people in Britain still describe themselves in class terms, and a majority still see themselves as working class
Source: *The Guardian*, 15 January 1999, p.3

Many sociologists argue that class has lost much of its significance for identity, some go so far as suggesting that 'class is dead' (Pakulski and Waters, 1996). The evidence offered for these claims mixes changing social and economic structures and the rise of other sources of identity and belonging. In the immediate post-war era, large-scale manufacturing and mining employed far more people than in the 1990s, and working-class identification was reflected in mass membership of organizations such as the Labour Party, trade unions, and work-based social and political clubs. Many of these organized sources of identity were dominated by, or exclusive to, men. The rise of mass unemployment in the 1970s and 1980s, the shift to service industries and the increase in the number of women working led to many of these institutions fragmenting, and membership dropped. An identification with work-based community cultures may have declined with it.

Other work-based structural changes reinforced this erosion of identities based on work. As national collective bargaining declined, trade unionism fragmented into more sectional identities. The Labour Party leadership worked hard in the 1990s to shed any identification of the party with the working class, seeking the 'middle' social ground. Work-based identities have also been cross-cut with other sources of identity. The rising importance of gender and ethnic identities and the emphasis in the mass media on diverse consumption-based lifestyles, has reinforced awareness that individuals play an active role in the construction of their own identity.

Social class is both a central and a highly contested concept within social science: there is little agreement over its meaning, measurement, or how it should be used as an explanatory device. However, as a field of social scientific inquiry, social class is dominated by two distinctive traditions of thought – Marxism and Weberianism. These traditions are rooted in the writings of Karl Marx (1818–1883) and Max Weber (1864–1920). While Marx and Weber differ in important ways in their understanding of class and society, both share a view of classes as groups structured out of economic relationships. Upon this central foundation, successive generations of social scientists have reworked and reformulated the arguments of Marx and Weber in the light of social, economic and political change. Each tradition brings together, in distinctive ways, an analysis of the economic roots of class, and a perspective on representation and the construction of class identities. The rest of this section explores some central ideas of these two living traditions within the social sciences.

5.2 The Marxist theory of class

Marx and his close associate Friedrich Engels were responsible for a theory of class that has been important both for its intellectual influence upon subsequent generations of social scientists, and for its wider political influence. Marx's ideas were a product of nineteenth century European and British society. When Marx was writing, European society was going through a period of profound upheaval and transformation. The Industrial Revolution had brought new industries and occupations to the ever-expanding towns and cities, where much of the working class population lived in dreadful conditions. This was also a period of profound political change, as newly emerging social groups struggled for power. Trade unions were developing, and the new industrial working classes increasingly fought for better working conditions, better housing and education, and political representation. Marx's theory of class reflects this period of social upheaval and conflict.

Marx's theory of **class** was part of a much wider project of explaining the historical emergence of industrial capitalism, as this new type of society was called, and its main driving forces. He saw the key defining feature of a society as being the way in which goods and wealth are produced. The organization and ownership of the means of production – tools, machines, workplaces and raw materials – shape the social relationships between individuals and groups within a society. The factories being constructed in mid-nineteenth century Britain were the means of production of the industrial capitalist system. The owners of capital, that is, of the financial wealth invested in the new manufacturing processes, were identified by Marx as the new ruling class.

Marx and class
For Marxists, class is rooted in the economic organization of production.

For Marx and Engels, capitalist society generated two main classes, or as they put it , 'two great warring and hostile camps' (Marx and Engels, 1848, p.49), a capital-owning class and a propertyless class, who occupied different positions in the organization of production. They called these classes the 'bourgeoisie' and the 'proletariat', or the ruling class and the working class. In return for their labours, the workers received a wage but the products of their labour were appropriated by capitalists and sold for profit, a process that Marx called *exploitation.*

There is much more that could be said about Marx's analysis of class but here we want to emphasize just three themes that have considerable continuing force in the way we think about class identities. First is the link between individual economic position within systems of production – specifically the ownership of capital – and class position. For Marx and later Marxists, class is a structure rooted in the economic organization of production.

Second is the idea of social polarization and associated class conflict. Marx expected that as capitalism developed, big business would gradually squeeze out all the small-scale capitalists, the self-employed and the small shop-owners. The result would be a growing divide between the bourgeoisie and a proletariat who were constantly threatened with impoverishment. Later industrial capitalism – at least in the more developed countries – has created a better-off and more differentiated workforce than this vision imagined. But scope for new forms of social polarization remains (see Section 7).

Class consciousness
An awareness of a shared class interest and of the existence of classes with opposing interests.

Third, Marx's emphasis on **class consciousness** is particularly relevant to our understanding of identity. Marx stressed class conflict in all his writings, but he did not see class conflict as inevitable. According to Marx, two factors were necessary for a fully developed proletarian class to exist: *objective* factors, that is, workers who share the same relationship to the means of production, and *subjective* factors. The latter refer to an awareness of a shared class position and of the existence of other classes with opposing class interests. This is how Marx describes the birth of the working class and its consciousness:

> Economic conditions had first transformed the mass of the people of the country into workers. The domination of capital has created for this mass a common situation, common interests. The mass is thus already a class against capital, but not yet for itself. In the struggle ... this mass becomes united, and constitutes itself as a class for itself. The interests it defends become class interests.
>
> (Marx and Engels, 1983, p.211)

Thus full class consciousness only emerges though the experience of solidarity and collective action. Marx put forward a strong notion of collective class identity which was rooted in economic structures that he saw as inherently conflictual, and developed through collective action in the experience of organization and class struggle.

Marxism, then, sees social relationships and human action as being constrained by the economic structures of society, but argues that those structures also generate the conditions for collective consciousness and identity. The development of a new type of society necessitates collective, not individual, action.

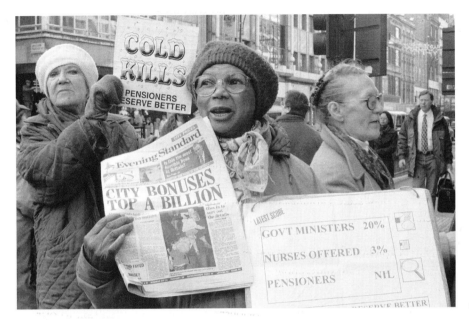

FIGURE 3.9 Solidarity and collective action: Members of the Greater London Pensioners Organization contrasting levels of city pay to the level of their pensions, January 1998

FIGURE 3.10 Solidarity and collective action: Tameside Care Group workers waving to supporters while demonstrating against government actions

5.3 Max Weber's theory of social stratification

Max Weber, one of the founders of the discipline of sociology, was writing at the time of the major social upheavals that gripped European societies just before and after the First World War. Weber's perspective, and the tradition of social analysis based upon it, offers an alternative vision of social class to that put forward by Marx.

Weber is credited with drawing attention to forms of *stratification* other than class, in particular to divisions of status and what he calls 'party'. 'Party', in Weber's writings, refers to any organization or voluntary association that brings together people with common backgrounds, aims or interests in pursuit of particular policies or control of a particular organization. (The relationship between 'party' and political power is explored more fully in **Hughes and Fergusson, 2004, Chapter 4**.) Like Marx, Weber recognizes the existence of economically defined social classes, but his starting point is individuals. In Weberian sociology, **class** refers to identifiable groups of individuals who have certain interests in common. These common interests can be summarized as market position, that is, individuals having similar opportunities for earning income through work or trade.

Weber and class
Weberians see class as being rooted in market position.

Different class groupings thus have distinct market situations which either privilege them or make them more vulnerable. Because of privileged access to the means of production and consumption, members of certain groups will enjoy better 'life chances' than others. Life chances refer to opportunities for education, health, housing, employment and levels of income. The key point is that for Weberians, class divisions and inequalities reflect different life chances in the market, whereas for Marxists, class relationships are founded in exploitative production relations.

Weber, like Marx, identifies a division between propertied and propertyless classes, but he also highlights divisions within those classes, divisions that are the product of differential reward by the market. For example, professional employees tend to find themselves in a privileged position in the market relative to semi-skilled workers. Markets operate in a way that divide and subdivide classes. As a result, the differentiation between groups of employees becomes increasingly complex.

Status
The prestige, honour or social standing attached to different social groups.

For Weber, this fragmentation of classes is accentuated by differences in **status**, that is, the different amount of prestige, honour or social standing that society attaches to different social groups. Thus status relies on people's subjective evaluation of social differences: '"Classes" are stratified according to their relations to the production and acquisition of goods; whereas "status groups" are stratified according to the principles of their consumption of goods as represented by special "styles of life"' (Weber, quoted in Hughes, 1984, p.8). Weber used the idea of lifestyle to describe the distinctive style of life of specific status groups. Within contemporary consumer society lifestyle has come to be associated with individuality and self-expression, for example through a range of activities based upon consumption of products and services.

Membership of a particular status group may confer certain benefits or rewards, or prohibit people from access to them. For example, members of different ethnic minority or religious groups may find themselves alternatively privileged or prohibited in this respect, *irrespective of their class position.* Hence, different groups may find themselves occupying similar economic class positions while being distinguished by differences in status, and status may be more significant than class as a source of identity. Groups may also experience inequalities in power deriving from party, that is, from the ability to organize themselves to further their own interests and to marginalize others. Weber thus sees class, status and party as cross-cutting, with class more concerned with the production of goods and status with their consumption. This vision of social fragmentation and increasing social diversity contrasts sharply with the Marxist image of class-based social polarization.

5.4 Class and identity in the two traditions

ACTIVITY 3.3

This activity asks you to try to apply these two traditions to an example of new types of paid work. Read the case study of call centres in Box 3.1 and then write some notes in answer to the following question.

How would social scientists in the tradition of (a) Marx and (b) Weber analyse the class position of call centre workers?

Try to bring issues of class consciousness and status into your argument.

BOX 3.1   Case study of call centres

Helplines, centralized telephone enquiry handling, direct sales and service, telephone banking, mortgage lending and insurance, teleconferencing: there was an explosion in the 1990s of large call centres handling all these types of telephone-based activity. Section 4 introduced the concept of capital investment as a major force structuring our working lives; call centres are an example of this. In the 1990s, new firms mushroomed to undertake direct selling and customer services, and existing firms invested large sums in centralizing or creating these activities, in order to reduce costs or fight off competition from new, wholly telephone-based companies such as *First Direct*. In the twenty-first century most of us can only access details of the account held at our local bank via the Internet or a distant call centre.

FIGURE 3.11   Answering calls at *First Direct*, Leeds

A call centre is basically a large room where people sit at banks of telephones making and answering calls. By 1997 call centres employed about 300,000 people; this is expected to grow to half a million – more than 2 per cent of the workforce – by the year 2000 (*Financial Times*, 29 November 1998). The jobs are concentrated in particular areas, including central Scotland, Tyneside and the West Country, where unemployment is high and labour is thought to be relatively cheap. A survey in Scotland in 1997 found 108 call centres, a third with over 500 employees, and plans for new large centres employing thousands (Taylor and Bain, 1999). Glasgow Development Agency is actively campaigning for call centre investment in the city.

Call centre employment, however, has a problematic reputation (Fernie and Metcalfe, 1997; *The Guardian*, 2 June 1998). Call centres have been called the 'new sweatshops' and 'white collar factories'. Call centre jobs are distinctive in the integration of telephone and computer technology: the 'agents' or 'representatives' answer queries and sell goods and services on the telephone while looking up and entering information on computer screens. New technology increases work rates: 'Dialling manually you can only make thirty calls and maybe speak to 10 people. The power dialler will get 80 phone calls and you'll speak to every one of them in a 4-hour shift' (quoted in Taylor and Bain, 1999).

Staff can see a display of the waiting calls stacked up for them, and they know that the time they take on calls and the money they bring in when selling are automatically monitored. The result is an 'assembly line in the head' (Taylor and Bain, 1999).

There are other forms of stress too. Staff have to work not only fast but pleasantly. They need to be 'natural' and to 'smile down the phone' – even when customers are rude or confusing. They need to follow a script, repetitively, while making each encounter seem personal to the caller. Staff are monitored not only by machine but also by supervisors listening in to their tone and manner. Some firms try to encourage 'teams' of employees to compete with each other. Some monitor, and even restrict, toilet visits.

The call centre workforce is predominantly young and female, and centres frequently organize shifts to fit round domestic activities. Wages are generally higher than, for example, shop counter jobs, but mental fatigue, voice-loss and depression are quite common, and turnover can be high – 30 per cent per year in some firms. Staff are generally set targets, for example for sales value per team per week (Taylor, 1998) and performance-related pay is quite common. Targets for speed and sales are often raised to increase pressure on staff.

One indicator of employees' resistance to some aspects of call centre work is unionization. Increasing numbers of call centres, especially the large ones, are unionized. Half of the Scottish centres in the 1997 survey had a union or a staff association. Unions trying to recruit, such as BIFU, CWU and Unison, have concentrated on work conditions (in one centre, it took unionization to get staff a tea break), health and safety at work, pay and holidays, rights for part-time staff (projected to be half the call centre workforce in Scotland by 2000), and limitations on uncontrolled monitoring of employees by supervisors.

COMMENT

There are a number of points you might have made in answer to the question. Here are just a few.

In the Marxist tradition, call centre employment would be analysed in terms of the relationship between the employer and the employee. In order to increase rates of work, new technology brings the pressures of the production line into 'white collar' work. A Marxist would see call centre workers as working class and point to rising discontent, resistance and unionization as evidence of growing class consciousness and a sense of collective work-place identity.

A Weberian would also identify elements of class: a group of individuals sharing a similar position in the labour force. Weberians might, however, highlight the use of mostly young female workers, stressing gender as a dimension of inequality of status affecting market position but not reducible to class. They might point to the emphasis on individual skill, internal competition between workers, and performance-related pay as fragmenting the workforce, and might see unionization as the pursuit of sectional interests rather than evidence of collective identity.

SUMMARY

- Both traditions see class and class divisions as rooted in economic structures.

- In Marxism, class is structured by the ownership and organization of production; in Weberianism, class is structured by market position.

- Class is more central to the Marxist tradition than to the Weberian tradition.

- Weberians identify non-class elements of social stratification, notably status and party, that are independent of social class.

- Class consciousness – involving identification as a member of a class – in the Marxist tradition emerges through collective action.

- Identity and collective action in the Weberian tradition focus more on status group than on class.

6 AN EROSION OF CLASS IDENTITY?

Section 5 began by considering some of the claims made about the extent of class divisions in the UK today. As we saw, a popular argument in both the social sciences and political debate is that the 'old' certainties of social class have been eroded. In the late 1990s, the issue of class was given renewed prominence by the Labour Prime Minister's claim that:

> Slowly but surely, the old establishment is being replaced by a new, larger, more meritocratic middle class.
>
> A middle class characterised by greater tolerance of difference, greater ambition to succeed, greater opportunities to earn a decent living.
>
> A middle class that will include millions of people who traditionally may see themselves as working class, but whose ambitions are far broader than those of their parents and grandparents.
>
> (Tony Blair, quoted in *The Guardian*, 15 January 1999, p.3)

Similar arguments have been made by sociologists and political scientists, not only in the 1980s and 1990s, but also in the 1950s and 1960s. Two claims recur: there has been a move from collective to individual identities and also there has been a move from occupation to consumption patterns as sources of social distinction.

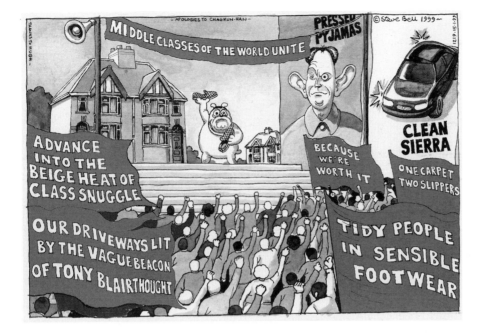

In the early 1960s, with the experience of a booming economy and rising consumption plus three general election victories for the Conservatives in 1951, 1955 and 1959, it was widely argued that well-paid sections of the working class were increasingly adopting middle-class values and lifestyles, thus eroding working-class identities. A study of attitudes and class identity among car workers at Vauxhall's Luton car plant (Goldthorpe *et al.*, 1969) concluded that there was little evidence to support these claims, but there were signs that working-class identity was fragmenting and a growing differentiation among a 'new' working class was developing.

The researchers argued that the new working class were distinguished by 'instrumentalism', that is, simply working for money. Work played a smaller role in their sense of identity than it did for the 'traditional' working class, with 'non-work' life, that is, family and home, playing a more important role. A sense of class identity, characteristic of the traditional working class, was being eroded by a more home-centred or 'privatized' and individualistic sense of identity. (That the Luton car workers went on strike only weeks after the study was completed failed to dispel claims that a 'new' working class was in the making.)

6.1 Class and consumption

The idea that class, as a structural factor shaping outlook on life and sense of social identity, was being replaced by non-work-based sources of identity reappeared vigorously in the 1980s and 1990s, once more in a context of widespread social and economic change and successive election victories for the Conservatives. Peter Saunders, an influential British sociologist, argued in the 1980s that consumption processes and differences in lifestyle had become more important than occupation-based class in constructing identities and in explaining social behaviours and attitudes (Saunders, 1984). In particular, he and others argued that the decline in votes for the Labour Party was largely due to the emergence of new consumption cleavages.

Voting preferences have long been identified by political scientists and sociologists as one of the key indicators for assessing the prevalence of *class identification*. The period following 1945 is said to be characterized by class alignment, that is, people tended to vote along class lines, with the working class predominantly voting Labour and the middle and upper classes opting for the Conservatives. Working-class Conservatives were seen as a puzzle requiring explanation. Conversely, Labour's declining share of the vote in the 1980s and early 1990s was attributed to class dealignment, reflecting an erosion of class and work-based sources of identity.

> **Class alignment**
> People tending to vote along class lines.

Saunders argued that a major process of 'social restratification' was taking place during this period, with a growing division between a 'middle mass' of those who could increasingly satisfy their consumption needs through private ownership of cars, housing and even private education and health care, and those who remained insecurely dependent on state provision of housing, public transport, education and health care. He predicted: 'an increasingly visible fault line in British society, not along the lines of class, but on the basis of private ownership of the means of consumption' (Saunders, 1984, p.211).

Saunders was not only arguing that new forms of stratification have emerged, but also that these are independent of work and class-based social divisions. Thus divisions of consumption and lifestyle cut across 'old' class lines, with consumption now influencing and shaping identity and social attitudes to a far greater extent.

Saunders' arguments were widely criticized for their failure to show that consumption directly influences people's identities and attitudes, such as political preferences. Critics noted that studies such as Saunders' continued to point to occupational class as a powerful influence on income, consumption and political attitudes and identities (Crompton, 1998).

Both the Luton researchers in the 1960s and Saunders in the 1980s claim that after 1945 UK society became increasingly individualized. The Luton study made this claim in a context of rising economic prosperity. By contrast, in the decades that followed, sociologists attributed individualization to the increasing insecurity of employment that forced individuals to negotiate their own path through unstable labour markets. So both prosperity and insecurity may lead to individualization and a move away from workplace-based identities, as illustrated in the John Greaves example in Chapter 1. In the 1980s, employment instability is argued to have eroded workplace and occupational communities, and forced people to see their working lives as unstable personal journeys. In place of collective work-based identities, individuals constructed their images of themselves much more around consumption and lifestyles.

Pierre Bourdieu, a French sociologist, has examined the interrelationship between class and consumption through empirical studies of consumption habits. In his book *Distinction*, Bourdieu explores the ways in which people express their identity through consumption (Bourdieu, 1984). Because consumption tastes are one way we distinguish ourselves from others, consumption patterns differentiate both *within* and *between* classes. In this way, he argues, consumption both establishes and expresses social difference. People invest effort as well as money in consumption, and two people with similar incomes but different economic class positions will be likely to have very different consumption patterns. Bourdieu's concept of cultural capital is linked to lifestyle. Social divisions do not rely only on the ownership or not of economic capital but also cultural capital, which cannot be reduced to economic factors. Economic capital does not guarantee what Bourdieu calls distinction or power in the social field. Cultural capital, which includes education and sports and leisure activities, has to have symbolic status and be recognized within the society as having high status. Bourdieu, who looks explicitly back to both Marx and Weber, sees occupational class and consumption as interrelated, not opposing, influences on identity.

ACTIVITY 3.4

Make a list of some ways in which consumption patterns and preferences differ between social classes, and consider how far we are able to make choices about consumption patterns.

COMMENT

You might have mentioned differences between working-class and middle-class people in television viewing habits, clothing and food preferences, musical tastes, home decoration, choice of cars and holidays. Note that Bourdieu, like other social scientists, is not arguing that all individuals conform to class-related consumption patterns; he is interested, rather, in the way that cultural practices such as consumption preferences are highly symbolic markers of status and class distinction. As a result, it can be hard for a member of a particular status or occupational group to sustain a consumption pattern very different from that expected of him or her. Finally, as Section 2 made clear, low incomes limit consumption choices very sharply indeed.

SUMMARY

- Class as a source of collective identity may be being eroded by a more individualistic and consumerist culture.

- Some sociologists argue that consumption has replaced class as the key factor structuring social division and identities.

- Sociologists such as Bourdieu also emphasize consumption as a major influence on identity, but analyse consumption as an expression of differentiation within and between classes.

7 SOCIAL POLARIZATION AND SOCIAL EXCLUSION

7.1 A polarizing society?

If you look back at the different understandings of inequality that have run through this chapter from Section 3 onwards, you can perhaps divide them into two camps. There is one set that sees inequality as gradations in a hierarchy. The 'income parade' fits in here: it shows how many more people live below than above average incomes, and how few and wealthy are the rich, but there are no sharp breaks in the parade. You might see Weber's complex mix of class position and status in the same light, and Bourdieu too: inequality in society is complex, and hierarchical, with cross-cutting identities. There are no sharp breaks.

Then there is the other camp: theorists who spot fault lines or cleavages, and emphasize conflict. These views are found right across the political spectrum; they include Marxists and also sociologists like Saunders who emphasize consumption cleavages. This image of a social divide re-entered the middle ground of UK politics in the late 1990s, with the Blair government's emphasis on the problem of **social exclusion**. The government's policies are underpinned by the argument that Britain displays a growing polarization between a relatively affluent majority and a large excluded minority.

Social exclusion
Some groups are marginalized and excluded from full participation and from taking advantage of all that is available to the more affluent in society.

Social polarization
A growing social divide between a relatively affluent majority and a large excluded minority.

Those arguing that there is **social polarization** do have some evidence on their side. In addition to the widening inequality, low wage rates and low benefit levels described in Sections 2 and 3, there has been a profound change in the distribution of work across households (Buck *et al.*, 1994; Gregg and Wadsworth, 1996; Harkness *et al.*, 1998). Since the early 1980s, the proportion of households with a single earner has declined sharply; households with more than one earner have increased in number. And, while in 1979 just 1 in 10 households had no paid earner, by 1994–5 this had increased to 1 in 5 (DSS, 1998, p.41). This emerging division between 'work poor' and 'work rich' households appears to interact with other influences in creating an 'excluded' group whose chances of getting into, or back into, paid employment are very low. Reflecting this, the new Office of National Statistics (ONS) social classification, which was referred to in the introduction to this chapter and illustrated in Figure 3.1, and which will be used in the 2001 census, has a new 'class 8' category for those who have never worked and are unlikely to do so.

Furthermore, while some of the so-called 'work rich' households have two professional earners and are well within the top tenth of the income distribution, many multiple-earner households cope on several low, insecure incomes. Unemployment remains high in the UK, and wages and insecurity of employment at the lower end have worsened. Relatively low-skilled work has become casualized, is predominantly female and displays a high rate of staff turnover (Pinch, 1993). Some of the call centre work discussed in Section 5 comes into this category (and call centres themselves may be superseded by new forms of technology, such as e-commerce, in a few years time). Data on household incomes over time shows that fluctuations and insecurity of incomes are far more prevalent among low income groups than among the better off. The experience of recurrent poverty affects many more than those who are poor at any one time (Gardiner and Hills, 1999).

Finally, the deterioration of public services and infrastructures in the 1980s and 1990s reinforced social polarization. Poverty and unemployment are geographically highly concentrated, notably in parts of the inner cities and on large housing estates. Higher charges and declining standards in public transport, education, housing and the health services have a cumulatively worse impact on those who rely on them most (see **Hughes and Fergusson, 2004**). Saunders' arguments have some leverage here: as the public sector deteriorates, it contributes to trapping those who cannot 'go private' into poverty.

There is some good economic evidence, then, for social polarization. However, the argument becomes much more problematic and contested when it moves from incomes and employment to culture and identity. Some commentators, (such as the influential US commentator Charles Murray) see social polarization as creating a so-called 'underclass'. They argue that such communities generate a distinct culture of resistance, characterized by criminality and avoidance of employment. This argument has been widely criticized as stigmatizing the disadvantaged. So do people have distinct identities, shaped by different attitudes to income and paid work, in 'excluded' communities?

7.2   Uncertainty and identity

At the end of the 1980s, the sociologist Bill Jordan and a group of colleagues set out to answer this question through detailed interviewing of families on one outer-city council estate in southern England. In their study *Trapped in Poverty?*, the researchers argue that the families they studied held ideas about what their roles should be in work and in the family that were no different from those of the rest of society. They did not see themselves as excluded or as members of an 'underclass'. What was different, however, was the difficulty of making sense of their work-related identities when faced with the economic pressures upon them.

The predominant experience of the interviewees was insecurity. A minority of men had regular long-term employment and they were all well aware of its value and its fragility. Almost all the men had been unemployed. All the men talked of needing to work, and idleness was characterized as boring and destructive of identity and self-respect (Jordan *et al.*, 1992, p.99). The men made sense of their lives through narratives about how they managed insecurity and the difficulty of finding work. In explaining how they saw themselves and their working lives, the men drew on familiar categories. They all, without exception, saw the proper role of a man as a breadwinner.

Men without regular work emphasized the importance of networks and knowledge in trying to find work. Some with irregular earnings characterized themselves as 'self employed', drawing on the language of enterprise and self-help – much emphasized by the politicians of the time – as a source of identity and self respect. Some men and women had bought or had discussed buying their homes, but this was as a source of stability and connection, not as a means of disconnection from the estate.

The women coped in similarly familiar terms. They emphasized women's primary responsibility for child care and household work, and drew on networks of female kin and friends to help them combine this with seeking employment. The vast majority of the households relied on women's contributions to total income, and in a minority of households women were the main earners. But even in the latter, women tended to emphasize their household role – even if they admitted to boredom with it – in explaining how they saw their approach to work. Some talked about 'spreading their wings' as the children got older, through employment and education.

The researchers emphasize that people on the estate were applying familiar norms and sources of identity to coping with a very difficult economic context. A good example is the attitude to casual work and unreported earnings. Both men and women were well aware of the problems posed by the benefits system for those trying earn a decent living: earning more or taking work could lead to benefits being withdrawn, so people got stuck in a 'trap' of poverty and unemployment. Everyone saw this as unfair and, as a result, regarded some undeclared cash work as normal and legitimate. But all constructed limits on how much it was 'fair' to earn and criticized (and occasionally informed on) those who drastically over-stepped the mark. The shared sense of fair, undeclared earnings was felt to be around £30-50 a week, well over the legal limit (£5 at the time), but far from extreme (Jordan *et al.*, 1992, p.319).

This resistance to legal rules – and the creation of informal local norms – was in the service of a work ethic and family responsibility, not as a method of avoidance. Note that the interviewers in this study were not seeking one 'true' story about what people do – perspectives differ within households, and some things may be hidden – but rather a sense of how people saw themselves in relation to paid work, how they would explain and justify themselves. The researchers found elements of collective identity – shared understandings and local forms of organizing to help people cope – and noted that the more secure households tended to have better patterns of kin support. They also found other patterns of stratification, notably differences between the households of regular workers and the rest. But they emphasized that there was no sharp distinction at all between the culture and identity of people on the estate and those reported elsewhere in the wider society.

SUMMARY

- Images of inequality differ between those that focus on gradations and those that focus on divides.
- There is good evidence for increasing social polarization in the contemporary UK in terms of incomes and employment experience.
- Economic insecurity is worst for those on low incomes.
- Research suggests that income-related and work-related identities do not greatly differ between poor and better off people.

8 CONCLUSION

Income and work are important sources of identity. But how the connection works between what we do and have and who we are changes over time. Our central theme in this chapter has been that economic structures, such as the extent of inequality and the nature of employment (which themselves change over time), interact with our understandings of who we are, and of what we can do and be.

Categories such as social class, consumption cleavages and social polarization are used by social scientists to understand the links between inequality of incomes and wealth and people's identity and behaviour. But those categories are also sources of identity: we still label ourselves frequently in class terms. And they are also political ideas: taken up by government and the media, they influence how we see ourselves – not least by leading us to protest!

Another theme of the chapter has been the relative and relational nature of work and income as sources of identity. All of the main concepts we have introduced – poverty, inequality, social class, consumption cleavages, social polarization and social exclusion – are about the economic position of some people relative to others, and about how some people are represented relative to others. Another way of saying this is that work-related identities are socially produced: we cannot have such identities except in relation to others.

REFERENCES

Adonis, A. and Pollard, S. (1998) *A Class Act*, Harmondsworth, Penguin.

Banks, J., Dilnot, A. and Low, H. (1996) 'Patterns of financial wealth holding in the United Kingdom', in Hills, J. (1996).

Beresford, P. and Croft, S. (1995) 'It's our problem too! Challenging the exclusion of poor people from poverty discourse', *Critical Social Policy*, 44–5, pp.75–95.

Blackwell, T. and Seabrook, J. (1996) *Talking Work*, London, Faber and Faber.

Bourdieu, P. (1984) *Distinction: a Social Critique of the Judgement of Taste*, London, Routledge and Kegan Paul.

Bradley, H. (1996) *Fractured Identities*, Cambridge, Polity.

Brown, M. (1988) *Richard Branson: the Authorised Biography*, London, Headline.

Buck, N., Gershuny, J., Rose, D. and Scott, J. (1994) *Changing Households: Household Panel Study 1990–92*, University of Essex Centre on Micro-Social Change.

Crompton, R. (1998) *Class and Stratification* (2nd edn), Cambridge, Polity.

Dean, H. (1992) 'Poverty discourses and the disempowerment of the poor', *Critical Social Policy*, vol.35, pp.79–88.

Department of Social Security (DSS) (1997) *Households Below Average Incomes: A Statistical Analysis 1979–1994–5*, London, The Stationery Office.

Fernie, S. and Metcalfe, D. (1997) '(Not) hanging on the telephone: payment systems in the new sweatshops', Centre for Economic Performance, London School of Economics.

Gardiner, K. and Hills, J. (1999) 'Policy implications of new data on income mobility', *Economic Journal*, vol.109, no.453, February, pp.F91–F111.

Goldthorpe, J., Lockwood, D., Bechhoffer, F. and Platt, J. (1969) *The Affluent Worker: Industrial Attitudes and Behaviour*, Cambridge, Cambridge University Press.

Goodman, A., Johnson, P. and Webb, S. (1997) *Inequality in the UK*, Oxford, Oxford University Press.

Gregg, P. and Wadsworth, J. (1996) 'More work for fewer households?' in Hills, J. (1996).

Harkness, S., Machin, S. and Waldfogel, J. (1982) 'Female employment and changes in the share of women's earnings in total family income in Great Britain' in Hedges, N. and Beynon, H. (1982) *Born To Work*, London, Pluto Press.

Hills, J. (1995) *Joseph Rowntree Foundation Inquiry into Income and Wealth,* vols. 1 and 2, York, Joseph Rowntree Foundation.

Hills, J. (ed.) (1996) *New Inequalities: the Changing Distribution of Income and Wealth in the United Kingdom,* Cambridge, Cambridge University Press.

Hughes, G. and Fergusson, R. (eds) (2004) *Ordering Lives: Family, Work and Welfare* (2nd edn), London, Routledge/The Open University.

Hughes, J. (1984) 'The concept of class' in Anderson, R. and Sharrock, W. (eds) *Teaching Papers in Sociology,* London, Longman.

Jenkins, S. and Cowell, F. (1994) 'Dwarfs and giants in the 1980s: trends in the UK income distribution', *Fiscal Studies,* vol.15, no.1, pp.99–118.

Jordan, B., James, S., Kay, H. and Redley, M. (1992) *Trapped in Poverty? Labour Market Decisions in Low Income Households,* London, Routledge.

Jowell, R., Curtice, J., Park, A., Brook, L. and Ahrendt, D. (1995) *British Social Attitudes: the 12th Report* (1995/96 edn), Aldershot, Dartmouth Publishing.

Kempson, E. (1996) *Life on a Low Income,* York, Joseph Rowntree Foundation.

Lister, R. and Beresford, P. (1991) *Working Together Against Poverty: Involving Poor People in Action Against Poverty,* Open Seminar Project, University of Bradford.

Marx, K. and Engels, F. (1848/1986) *Manifesto of the Communist Party,* Moscow, Progress Publishers.

Marx, K. and Engels, F. (1983) *Collected Works,* vol.VI, Moscow, Progress Publishers.

Office of National Statistics (ONS) (1998) *Social Trends,* 28, (1998 edition) London, The Stationery Office.

Pakulski, J. and Waters, M. (1996) *The Death of Class,* London, Sage.

Pinch, S. (1993) 'Social polarisation: a comparison of evidence from Britain and the United States', *Environment and Planning,* vol.25, no.6, pp.779–95.

Saunders, P. (1984) 'Beyond housing classes: the sociological significance of private property rights in means of consumption', *International Journal of Urban and Regional Research,* vol.8, no.2, pp.202–27.

Scott, J. (1994) *Poverty and Wealth,* London, Longman.

Sen, A.K. (1981) *Poverty and Famines,* Oxford, Clarendon Press.

Social Trends, London, The Stationery Office for Office for National Statistics (annual).

Taylor, P. and Bain, P. (1999) '"An assembly line in the head": work and employee relations in the call centre', *Industrial Relations Journal,* vol.30.

Tayor, S. (1998) 'Emotional labour and the new workplace' in Thompson, P.O. and Warhurst, C. (eds) *Workplaces of the Future,* London, Macmillan.

FURTHER READING

On inequality: John Hill's report to the Joseph Rowntree Foundation, *Inquiring into Income and Wealth*, vols. 1 and 2, is written for a general audience, and is very readable. It has a lot more on the income parade.

Fran Abrams (2002) *Below the Breadline*, London, Profile Books, offers a more recent discussion of poverty in the UK.

Polly Toynbee (2003) *Hard Work: Life in Low Pay Britain*, London, Bloomsbury, presents an accessible account of the experiences of people on very low wages.

On social class: Rosemary Crompton's book, *Class and Stratification* (1998) is a fairly accessible survey.

On consumption: Edgell, S., Hetherington, K. and Warde, A. (eds) (1996) *Consumption Matters*, Oxford, Blackwell, can be recommended.

Harriet Bradley (1996) *Fractured Identities,* Cambridge, Polity, is a useful discussion of interrelationship between class and gender.

Gerth, H. and Mills, C.W. (1948) *From Max Weber,* London, Routledge – has excerpts from original texts by Weber and useful introductory commentary.

Karl Marx, *Communist Manifesto* – the real thing. Clear polemic which highlights key parts of Marxist mystique. A good read!

A N S W E R   TO ACTIVITY 3.2

A single person needed to earn £22,000 to get into the top tenth. A couple with children where only one adult was earning needed over £50,000. But a childless couple each earning £17,000 would get in.

'Race', 'ethnicity' and identity

Gail Lewis and Ann Phoenix

Contents

1 INTRODUCTION

In this chapter, we look at the ways in which 'race' and 'ethnicity' are part of identity. We address three central questions:

- How can we understand the terms 'race' and 'ethnicity'?
- What is the relationship between identities we feel are central to us and those that other people 'read off' from (or ascribe to) us?
- Are 'race' and 'ethnicity' important to our identities even if we do not think they are?

In order to answer these questions we need to revisit the three questions posed at the beginning of Chapter 1 and make them relevant to identities of 'race' and 'ethnicity'. You may remember that these questions were:

- How are identities formed?
- How much control do we have in shaping our own identities?
- Are there particular uncertainties about identity in the contemporary UK?

In this chapter we use these questions to guide our discussion of 'race' and 'ethnicity'.

Over the course of the chapter we will provide support for three claims made in Chapter 1. Firstly, that how we see ourselves can be very different from how others see us and this may lead to conflicts in identities. We explore this claim by considering why it is important to understand how 'racial' and 'ethnic' identities are formed. Secondly, the organization of society is important in shaping our identities. Here we consider examples where fixed ideas of what it means to belong to a particular 'race' or 'ethnicity' are challenged. Thirdly, the social changes that have made the UK the multi-ethnic society it is have led to uncertainties and insecurities about identities as well as opportunities for the formation of new identities. We examine this claim by looking briefly at some of the factors influencing the emergence of new 'racial' and 'ethnic' identities and by examining whiteness as a 'racial' identity.

2 HOW ARE IDENTITIES OF 'RACE' AND 'ETHNICITY' FORMED?

Let us start by examining what social scientists have to say about how we come to have identities based on 'race' and 'ethnicity'. There are important social changes in how people think about 'race' and 'ethnicity' and these identities are not fixed. Group identities change as a result of collective action, even though people who are considered to be in the same 'racial' and 'ethnic' groups do not necessarily share the same identities. One reason for this is that 'racial' and 'ethnic' identities are not the only identities anybody has.

2.1 Questioning ideas that 'race' and 'ethnicity' are fixed categories

What do we mean by the terms 'race' and 'ethnicity'? These are commonly used in everyday life and in the media, but their meanings are rarely discussed.

ACTIVITY 4.1

Think about the terms 'ethnicity' and 'race'. What do they mean to you? Jot down the first things that come to mind and keep your notes so that you can think about them again as you read the chapter.

COMMENT

Thinking about how we currently use and understand particular terms can help us to see what we take for granted about them. We often expect that everyday terms have clear, consistent meanings. However, the words 'ethnicity' and 'race' are used in many different ways. For example, some people use them interchangeably, without making distinctions between them. Other people use them only to refer to people who are black or Asian or who they consider to have cultures that differ from what they understand to be British or English culture. In recent years, some people have come to prefer to use the term 'ethnicity' because they feel that it sounds more polite than 'race' and is less likely to be controversial. Whatever you wrote down, our understandings of terms affect the representations we have about the people or things to which they refer. These understandings also affect how we see ourselves. It is because of this that the ways in which we perceive 'race' and 'ethnicity' (as well as gender) have been much debated and have changed over time. The next section considers in more detail the meanings of the terms 'race' and 'ethnicity' and how they have changed in recent years.

2.2 What do social scientists mean by 'race' and 'ethnicity'?

Social scientists who study 'racial' and 'ethnic' identities partly base their theories on how different people think of themselves and how these identities have changed over time. A good illustration of this can be seen in the way the term 'black' has been used in the UK and in the USA. In both places it has changed from being viewed as a term of contempt to being one of pride. Henry Louis Gates, an African American professor of literature, puts this idea clearly at the beginning of his autobiography: 'The "Personal Statement" for my Yale [university] application began: "My grandfather was colored, my father was Negro, and I am black"' (Gates, 1994, p.201). In the UK, the term 'black' also came to be widely used in the 1970s. Initially, it was used to refer only to black people of African descent. However, in the 1980s, in the UK (but not USA) it also came to be used to include people of Asian descent. Yet, by the end of the 1980s, it had moved back to its initial, more restricted meaning. In both the UK and the USA, people with one black and one white parent were included within the category black until the 1990s. However, as the numbers of people who are recognizably of 'mixed parentage' have increased, many now wish to be recognized as 'mixed', rather than 'black' or 'white'. It is clear then, that the terms, 'black', 'Asian' and 'mixed parentage' change over time. They are *dynamic* rather than static. Why should this be the case?

Most importantly, shifts have occurred because definitions of these terms are, and have been, much disputed. What groups should be called, who has the right to define them and who should be included within particular terms have all been hotly debated because they describe and define unequal social power relations as well as similarities and differences between people. 'Black' came into popular usage because many people of African origin (including those from the Caribbean) in the USA and in the UK subscribed to the ideas of the Black Power, black consciousness and civil rights movements. They insisted that blackness should not be considered shameful, but should be reclaimed as a source of pride and beauty. As a result, they argued, being called 'black' was no more insulting than being called 'white' and was preferable to the euphemistic 'coloured'. The change in terminology thus involved collective group action and resistance to the way in which white people (the more powerful group) had viewed and defined black people. The appearance of the Black Power and black consciousness movements in the 1960s makes clear that it is possible for there to be dramatic changes in identifications and identities over a lifetime and between different generations. The very notion of what it means to be black and to have a black identity changes as political and social science ideas change (Gilroy, 1994). This is why we argue that it makes better social science sense to think of black identities as diverse and changing, rather than as singular and fixed. Let's take a moment to explore this idea further.

We can apply to this example Goffman's sociological idea (introduced in Chapter 1) of performance and the idea that information 'given off' unintentionally is read and interpreted by others. For instance, we can see that black people began to perform being black differently (as a source of pride) and insisted that the meaning 'given off' by the cue of colour should no longer be considered shameful and inferior, but as signifying equal worth. It was a struggle to alter the social meaning of blackness.

The example of black people's shift to insisting that 'Black is Beautiful' is also much used to illustrate Social Identity Theory, which argues that less powerful groups seek to improve their social position, making their social identity more positive in relation to the more powerful group. The 'Black is Beautiful' slogan is an example of a strategy called 'social creativity' which involves a positive redefinition of the social identity of black people (the less powerful group) in comparison with white people (the more powerful group) and so calls for social change in an innovative way. Identities are, therefore, collective and political as well as individual.

FIGURE 4.1   'Black is Beautiful'

The 'Black is Beautiful' example also demonstrates two other theoretical points about identities introduced in Chapter 1. Firstly, that they are relational. Secondly, since identities are not fixed, they cannot be a source of certainty throughout time and in all circumstances.

ACTIVITY 4.2

Stop for a moment and look back at what you have just read about the changing meaning of blackness. Now that you have done this, jot down a few notes in response to:

- what it means to say that identities are relational
- why shifting identities might be a potential source of uncertainty.

COMMENT

The changes in the meaning of the term black were a response to how being black was viewed as inferior in relation to being white. This shows that the meaning of blackness is created through its relation to – and difference from – whiteness. So too the meaning of whiteness is created through its relation to and difference from blackness. The insistence by black people that 'Black is Beautiful' was very positive for black people. They were making a collective claim for equal social worth and so were unsettling established ideas about what it meant to be black *and* to be white. At first sight it might appear that this change would have little impact on white people. However, their taken-for-granted certainty that they were superior to black people was destabilized, with the result that their racialized identities became more uncertain than previously. For both groups, 'who they were' was defined in relation to one another. Yet for both groups uncertainty was signalled by the very fact that 'who they were' had changed.

How then did people living in the UK in the late twentieth century deal with changes in the term black? People from a variety of different regions, including Africa, the Caribbean and the Indian sub-continent have collectively negotiated the problems of racism. Because of the similarities in the experiences of African, Caribbean and Asian people in the UK, the term 'black' was expanded to include people of South Asian descent in the 1970s when the different groups joined forces so that they could better oppose racism. This shared experience was asserted in relation to white people. However, it was also defined in relation to African, Asian and Caribbean British people.

This form of inclusive 'black' identity was specifically British. Its roots lay in a shared experience of both British colonialism and contemporary racism. It was coming to the UK that produced a black identity and, in much the same way, coming to the UK produced a Caribbean identity for people from the Caribbean who had, previously, been 'more divided by island allegiances they had left behind than united by a racial identity they were coming to share'

(Younge, 2002, p.30). ' ... the whole experience of living in a white racist society has helped to forge a black identity where in many cases such an identity did not exist previously' (James, 1993, p.243).

However, from the end of the 1980s in the UK, the new term 'black and Asian' began to replace the more inclusive use of 'black'. Those who argued for the term 'black and Asian' did so for three reasons. Firstly, that 'black' in 'Black Power' referred to people of African descent. Secondly, that many South Asians did not identify as black and nor did many African Caribbeans recognize them as black. Thirdly, that the use of an all inclusive collective category led to Asian people's needs not being recognized and met (e.g. their needs for resources from local and/or central government) (Brah, 1996).

Not only is black identity built in relation to whiteness, it is also produced in relation to what it is to be Asian. In addition, it is not possible to be complacent about what constitutes black identity since this is subject to change and can produce tensions between how people see themselves and how others see them. This example also shows that such tensions may be linked to questions of access to resources.

Changes in ideas about how blackness should be thought about led to increased understanding that there are different forms of racism. For this reason, it is now generally accepted that **racisms** have to be seen as plural (Brah, 1996). Racisms range from the grossest practices of genocide and slavery, through harassment and denial of social rights, to name-calling. They involve exclusion and, frequently, treating people as if they are inferior. Racisms are, therefore, intimately connected with power relations since one group has to have the power to exclude another from power and resources. Here are just a few illustrations of the wide-ranging forms of racism.

Racisms
The varied forms of racism that affect many different groups of people who are identified as belonging to 'races' not considered to be socially valuable. Racisms can involve obvious practices of genocide and discrimination as well as more subtle denials of social rights or name-calling.

'NO COLOUREDS'

To Let: Decent single bed-sitting room with facilities to cook in basement kitchen. Suit a working gentleman or woman. Only respectable people need apply. No coloureds please.

(Advert in Southall Shop, 1958, cited in Campaign Against Racism and Fascism/ Southall Rights, 1981, p.8)

RACIST ABUSE

RP: 'Does that happen now at all that you're called Paki?'

Zac: 'Um, um, no, not, it doesn't happen as often as it used to. Yeah, because, um, like say if I was to be on the street, it'll still happen because, if they see, if you're brown, they'll assume that, they'll call you a Paki yeah and they'll start pickin' on you because – I was up the park wiv my mate yeah, he was Pakistan or Muslim, I dunno what really. And these kids just came up to him and they knew I was Hindu and they tried to pick on him cos they thought he was a Paki.'

(Zac, 13-year-old British Asian boy talking to interviewer, in Frosh *et al.*, 2002, pp.171–2)

NO JUSTICE – THE MURDER OF STEPHEN LAWRENCE

The wall of silence [surrounding his murder] was not only in the surrounding area where my son was killed but with the police officers who were supposed to be investigating the crime. What I have seen and heard in the last three days only confirms what I have been saying all along. Right from the start, the night our son was murdered, it seems that in the minds of the police he was only a black boy, why bother. No-one can convince me otherwise, the evidence is clear to see by the action they took or didn't take.

(Doreen Lawrence, mother of Stephen, in her statement after the Inquest in February 1997, cited in the Report of the Stephen Lawrence Inquiry: The Stationery Office, 1999, p.300)

INSTITUTIONAL RACISM

The collective failure of an organisation to provide an appropriate and professional service to people because of their colour, culture, or ethnic origin. It can be seen or detected in processes, attitudes and behaviour which amount to discrimination through unwitting prejudice, ignorance, thoughtlessness and racist stereotyping which disadvantage minority ethnic people.

(The Stephen Lawrence Inquiry: The Stationery Office, 1999, p.28)

What each of these examples shows is that racisms start from assumptions about individuals and groups on the basis of colour, culture or some other attributes. To put it another way, racisms start by a process of 'reading off' from people's bodies, names, languages or forms of dress. Individuals or organizations then use these markers as the basis for unequal access to resources or treatment.

How does this history of changes in 'racial' and 'ethnic' identities and therefore in the terms used to refer to 'race' and 'ethnicity' help us to expand our understanding of how these identities are formed? We have seen that 'racial' and 'ethnic' identities are produced as part of a social process, that they are collectively produced and that they may change over time. Black people successfully took control of shaping how they wanted to define their identities. However, the fact that they needed to do this indicates that their identities were constrained by racism in their societies. The changes in who is included and who is excluded from black identities show that we are not entirely free to choose our 'racial' identities. Our identities are thus produced from a negotiation between those identities we adopt and those that other people ascribe to us.

SUMMARY

- 'Racial' and 'ethnic' categories are not fixed and the meanings attached to them change so that they are different in different contexts.
- 'Racial' identities are relational.
- Social scientists have paid increasing attention to both the construction of 'racial' and 'ethnic' identities and of the boundaries between them.
- Racisms take many different forms.

2.3 Racialization and ethnicization

You may have noticed that every time we have used the words 'race', 'racial' or 'ethnic' we have put them in quotation marks. Many social scientists put 'race' into quotation marks to show that it does not refer to clear biological differences, but is made significant in social practices. For that reason, many social scientists use the terms 'racialized', 'racialization', 'ethnicized' and 'ethnicization' instead of 'race' and 'ethnicity'. At first reading you may find these alternative words awkward and may even fail to see how they are different or why they are important. They are different from the terms 'race' and 'ethnicity' in two main ways. Firstly, 'racialization' and 'ethnicization' place an emphasis on the social and psychological processes involved in putting individuals and groups into 'racial' or 'ethnic' categories. Secondly, this means that the terms 'race' and 'ethnicity' are no longer seen to be natural or fixed, but as identities that result from particular ways of seeing people. Let us look at how three people describe their racialized identities to make this point clearer.

> I was accepted as a white person in Trinidad. For all practical purposes, I am coloured in England.
>
> (Gomes, 1973, 'I am an immigrant', cited in James, 1993, p.239)

> When we came here we swore we were English because Guyana was British Guiana. ... When you came here, you discovered it's a different thing. If you're English, you have to be white.
>
> (Mrs C., oral testimony, in Webster, 1998, p.44)

> When I was younger, living in an all-black neighborhood the other kids thought I was better than them because of my light skin and straight hair, then we moved to an all-white neighborhood and that was a culture shock. I'd been used to being around all black kids ... I'm black, I realized very early in my life that I wasn't going to be this mulatto stuck in the middle, not knowing if I'm black or white.
>
> (US actress Halle Berry, quoted in *Celebrity Movie Stars*, 2002)

These three people all talk about changes in how they saw their racialized or ethnicized identities. For all of them, the changes were the result of their responses to how they understood other people to see them. None of them could take their 'race' and 'ethnicity' for granted as natural or fixed. Instead, all their identities changed because of how they were categorized by other people. We can, therefore, see that social and psychological processes were important parts of the process of how their racialized and ethnicized identities were formed.

Before reading on, look back at the notes you made for Activity 4.1. It is likely that you emphasized things such as skin colour, facial features, or hair texture when thinking about 'race', and perhaps things such as culture, religion, or language for 'ethnicity'. It may be that you found it difficult to distinguish between 'race' and 'ethnicity'. Whatever ideas you came up with, it is worth considering whether you thought of these terms as taking their meaning in relation to other groups; for example, did you think of what it might mean to talk of 'the black race' in relation to 'the white race'? Or for 'ethnicity' did you think of what it might mean to talk of the 'ethnic minorities' in relation to 'the English' or 'the British'? If so, this connects with our suggestion that a more helpful way to think of 'race' and 'ethnicity' is in terms of *social processes*. We say more about this in what follows. Let us begin by exploring the terms 'ethnicity' and 'race' a little further.

'*Ethnicity*' refers to a group or community that is assumed to share common cultural practices and history. Religion, language and territory are all included in the term 'ethnicity'. It is, to a large extent, defined by the people who feel they belong to the group. 'Ethnic group' is sometimes used as if it refers only to people who are in less powerful positions within society and who are often subjected to racism. However, 'ethnicity' is a concept that refers to everybody so that, although many people use the word 'ethnic' as if it only refers to black or Asian people, it is equally relevant to white people. For that reason 'majority ethnic group' is sometimes used to refer to 'ethnic' groups which have relatively more power because their cultural practices and presence is taken for granted as natural in a society. If you are white, English and Christian (but not if you are Irish or Jewish) you are a member of the 'majority ethnic group' in Britain. The counterpart term 'minority ethnic group' refers to those groups whose cultural practices and history make it likely that they will be less powerful within a society. In the UK and the USA, 'majority ethnic' groups are white, but there are also white (as well as black) 'minority ethnic' groups, and in apartheid South Africa, the black 'minority ethnic' group was the numerical majority population. This potential contradiction between numerical status and power as minority and majority has proved confusing. As a result the majority/minority 'ethnic' group distinction has been much criticized for the ways in which many people confuse it with numerical proportions, rather than power relations as well as for its pejorative overtones.

In popular usage, many people believe that those who are considered to belong to the same 'race' belong to the same human stock. '*Race*' is seen as inherited and thought to be visible in physical difference. Skin colour, physical features, culture or territory have all been used as markers of the boundaries between 'races' (Anthias, 1996). However, as long ago as the 1930s, geneticists were arguing that these markers of 'race' are not clear indicators of biological difference. For this reason some people have argued that the term 'race' should not be used. Others put it into quotation marks to signify that it is socially constructed, rather than about 'natural' or biological difference. They argue that, although 'race' is a social construct, it has real effects: it continues to be treated as socially significant because inequalities are reproduced through practices of racism. The fact that it has real effects means that it is also important to identity. As you have seen, we adopt the use of quotation marks for both 'race' and 'ethnicity' for these reasons.

Imagine that you are describing yourself to someone from a very different country. Spend a few minutes thinking about how you would describe your own 'ethnicity' and 'race'.

Since there are problems with the ways in which both 'ethnicity' and 'race' have been defined and are used, neither term can be considered more apt or accurate than the other. Consequently, researchers on 'race' and 'ethnicity' have focused on the *processes* they involve rather than identifying fixed characteristics of particular groups. 'Ethnicity' and 'race' are about the process of marking differences between people on the basis of assumptions about human physical or cultural variations and the meanings of these variations. This is what we mean when we say that individuals and groups are racialized or ethnicized. The passport example discussed in Section 2 of Chapter 1 is a good example of how national identity involves including some people as the same as 'us' and excluding others as different. Having a particular passport means that a boundary is constructed between those who hold the same passport (and are constructed as having the same national identity) and those who do not (and so are constructed as having a different national identity). In much the same way, racialized and ethnicized identities are about setting and maintaining boundaries between groups.

One term, or concept, that captures this is 'racialization'. This was first used by the Martiniquan (French Caribbean) psychiatrist Franz Fanon in the early 1960s and has been taken up widely as a useful way of looking at the identities associated with 'race' (Fanon, 1967). This does similar work to the use of quote marks around 'race' in emphasizing that it is not naturally occurring. In addition, however, racialization indicates that 'race' is dynamic and that it becomes socially significant through various social, economic, cultural, or indeed psychological processes. The concept 'ethnicization' indicates dynamic processes that serve to put people into one 'ethnic' group or another on the basis of assumptions about culture, national origin, or language.

Because the terms racialize and ethnicize emphasize processes it becomes easier to see that people who are considered to belong to the same

Racialization
The dynamic processes that make 'race' socially, economically and psychologically significant.

Ethnicization
The dynamic processes that construct people as belonging to a particular 'ethnic' group on the basis of assumptions about culture, national origin, or language.

ethnicized group do not necessarily share the same social characteristics. Nor are they necessarily different from people who are considered to belong to other ethnicized groups. If we treat an 'ethnic' group or 'race' as if it has characteristics that infallibly make it different from other groups and as if all members of the group share all those characteristics, we are treating them in ways that have come to be referred to as essentialist. It is called **essentialism** (a term you first encountered in Chapter 2) because it treats groups as if they have a fundamental, fixed essence. This exaggerates differences and understates similarities between groups as well as treating members of the same group as if they are all the same and so erasing differences among them. One effect can be that attempts to recognize cultural differences may result in fixed and rigid views of culture.

Essentialism
This is a process that treats groups as if they have a fundamental essence, and so exaggerates differences and reduces similarities between groups while understating differences within groups.

An example of essentialist ideas about particular 'ethnic' groups is found in some research carried out in the UK with black women social workers. In this example, an interviewee describes an incident in which a social work team manager assumed that a child is from a particular 'ethnic' or 'racial' group on the basis of fixed and rigid views of cultural practices. The social worker says:

> [There] was a white woman who had been a manager ... and she had very racist opinions which she covered up, or tried to cover up ... I can remember one case in particular, where there was a young child whose mother was suffering from domestic violence. The parents weren't married, and she assumed that the child was black, which was an on-going thing with her. ... and she made some remark about ... 'Oh it's what *they* do ... it's just normal ...' I asked her what do you mean, what do you mean! ... . [She said] 'Well you know West Indian families, you know it's not too unusual ...' That kind of remark! Well I just flipped a lid and I said what are you talking about! Abuse and violence are not normal patterns of life, ... '[And anyway] she has got blonde hair and blue eyes, just like you' ... and the shock that came onto her face ... .

(Lewis, 2000, pp.139, 141, 142)

Stop for a moment and think of any examples where assumptions about a person's 'race' or 'ethnicity' have been made. What characteristics were used as the basis of the assumptions?

The creation of identity positions on the assumption of fundamental essences or characteristics can prevent people from seeing that there are *shared* cultural practices across 'ethnic' groups. This is shown in the example below taken from work in the Netherlands by Philomena Essed.

> A nineteen-year-old from Amsterdam is angry because she has to be home earlier than most of her classmates. She complains that her parents are overprotective, and she wants to move out, but she isn't quite sure how to do this without a huge fight. She is Turkish. She thinks that her parents are strict with her because they are Turkish. This image is reinforced by stories in the paper

about Muslim immigrants who are strict with their daughters and about girls who run away because they refuse to accept this any longer.

At a summer job, she works with an outgoing, slightly older Dutch girl. Imagine her surprise when this new friend vividly describes the fights she has had with her parents, their struggles, and the tricks she had to pull in order to move out. Imagine the Turkish girl's relief that over-protectiveness is not the prerogative of Turkish parents. She recognizes the experience she shares with her Dutch friend, even though she knows that there are also differences in the way they were raised.

(Essed, 1996, p.35)

In this second example, the young Turkish woman's essentialist ideas about Turkish parents are challenged by her friend's experience. However, 'insiders' to a group can sometimes insist that all members of a group should behave in the same ways and identify in the same ways. This belief underpins insults such as 'bounty' or 'coconut' applied to black people, or 'banana' for people of Chinese descent because they are seen to have failed to be black (or 'yellow') through and through.

Recognizing that racialized and ethnicized identities can be treated in essentialist ways reinforces the claim that there can be tensions between how people see themselves and how they are seen by others. It also indicates that there are a variety of ways in which people deal with the same identity positions. People who apparently have the same identity position (e.g. because they are all black) may well have very different identities. Fixed constructions of identity thus cannot do justice to those who are supposed to fit within them. The terms racialization and ethnicization help to alert us to the importance of being sceptical about claims that people have certain fixed characteristics.

Let us now take stock of what racialization, ethnicization and essentialism mean for racialized and ethnicized identities. We have seen how the very existence of essentialism means that how we see our identities is not necessarily how others see us. Essentialism means that other people can racialize and ethnicize us in ways that simplify and limit the identities we have. Yet, since other people do set up identity positions for us to occupy, our racialized and ethnicized identities are partly formed in relation to the identities ascribed to us. We can, however, choose either to take up or not to take up these ascribed identities and so, as we saw in the previous sub-section, we have some control in the shaping of our identities even though other people (including the state and local authorities) impose constraints on us.

S U M M A R Y

- Racialized identities are diverse.
- Essentialist notions of identity can prevent us from seeing what is the same about people of different 'ethnicities' and what is different about people within the same 'ethnic' groups.
- Essentialism may also result in unequal access to resources or different treatment by service providers.

2.4 How racialization and ethnicization intersect with other identities

Before you read this section it may be useful to look back at the section summaries in Chapter 1 in order to refresh your memory of the concepts developed there.

All the chapters you have read so far have demonstrated that everybody has many different identities all at the same time. Racialized and ethnicized identities therefore do not exist in isolation from other identities. This is nicely demonstrated in a famous speech given in 1851 by Sojourner Truth at the Women's Rights Convention in Akron, Ohio. Sojourner Truth was born into enslavement (to a wealthy Dutch slave-owner living in New York). She campaigned for both the abolition of slavery and for equal rights for women. Since she was illiterate throughout her life, no formal record of the speech exists and, indeed, two different versions of it are in existence (Gates and McKay, 1997). The words of Sojourner Truth had an enormous impact at the Convention and the challenge they express foreshadowed campaigns by black feminists more than a century later.

ACTIVITY 4.3

Read the following extract from Sojourner Truth's speech and, as you do so, note the identities she claims and how these make a challenge to essentialist thinking. In doing so, you need to be aware that there is an important identity that she takes for granted and expects her audience to take for granted because she is speaking in that context.

> Well, children, where there is so much racket, there must be something out of kilter, I think between the Negroes of the South and the women of the North – all talking about rights – the white men will be in a fix pretty soon. But what's all this talking about? That man over there says that women need to be helped into carriages, and lifted over ditches, and to have the best place everywhere. Nobody helps me any best place. And ain't I a woman? Look at me! Look at my arm. I have plowed, I have planted and I have gathered into barns. And no man could head me. And ain't I a woman? I could work as much, and eat as much as any man – when I could get it – and bear the lash as well! And ain't I a woman? I have borne

children and seen most of them sold into slavery, and when I cried out with a mother's grief, none but Jesus heard me. And ain't I a woman?

(Sojourner Truth, 1851, see

http://www.fordham.edu/halsall/mod/sojtruth-woman.html, accessed February 2003)

COMMENT

Throughout her speech, Sojourner Truth takes for granted that she is a 'Negro' and that everyone in the room sees this as her most important identity. Her speech does not unsettle white racialized identities. However, she does challenge her audience's gender identities. She claims an identity as a woman through repetition of the rhetorical question 'ain't I a woman?' She makes this strong identity claim of similarity to white women while pointing out that she has not been treated in the ways that white men and women considered symbolize womanhood. However, she also claims an identity of someone who is as strong as a man. Her short speech powerfully challenged essentialist thinking that women are necessarily weaker than men and that enslaved black women were not real women. Her identity claim is thus relational, constructed in relation to white women and all men and clearly demonstrates that identities involve power relations – in this case of inequality. In addition, her speech shows how racialized and gendered identities cannot be separated since everybody has both a gendered and a racialized position.

Since the identity positions that are available for people to take up are multiple and intersect with each other (as in the above example of the intersection of 'race' and gender) one person can have several identities related to the different social positions they occupy. Far from having a fixed, essential identity then, people have several identities that can change over time. To get an idea of what this means think about yourself. How many identities would you describe yourself as having? And because people take up identity positions in different ways, there are also a variety of similarities and differences between the identities of people occupying different social positions. Sojourner Truth's speech is likely to have changed how many white women thought about what it meant to have an identity of 'woman' and of 'white woman'. They may, for example, have started to include black women in the overall category 'woman', rather than seeing it as exclusively white with black women as a separate category. If so, they would have perceived similarities between themselves and black women of which they were previously unaware. Sojourner Truth's speech may have helped to change

FIGURE 4.2 Sojourner Truth

how white women (and men) constructed boundaries around the identity of 'woman'.

How does this discussion help us to answer the questions with which we started this chapter? As we have seen, Sojourner Truth was active in constructing her identity. She made a strong claim to being a woman like white women, even though the social context constrained her ability to be treated as white women were. She thus had some control over her racialized and ethnicized identity. Yet, it is clear that the society in which she lived, built as it was on racism, very much limited how she could express her identity. We also saw that claims to particular identities can make other people uncertain about their own identities. This example also shows that identities are formed in relation not just to other people, but also in relation to other identities. Thus, racialized identities are formed in relation to gendered and other identities.

SUMMARY

- Racialized and ethnicized identities intersect with other aspects of identity.
- Everyone has multiple identities.
- Since identities are relational, when people from one racialized or ethnicized grouping make identity claims these can help to unsettle the identities of people in other groups.

3 EVERYDAY RACIALIZED AND ETHNICIZED IDENTITIES

'Just now everybody wants to talk about "identity"' says the cultural studies analyst Kobena Mercer (1990, p.43). One result of this widespread concern with identity is that identities can be seen, and are generated, in the common everyday things we do. As we have seen, however, the ubiquity and ordinariness of identities does not mean that they are stable or secure.

3.1 Uncertain identities

Mercer puts the current focus on identity down to the uncertainty and diversity that characterizes modern identity. We can also link the heightened concern about racialized and ethnicized identities to another feature of contemporary life. This is the impact of large-scale migration of people and rapid social and technological change and the uncertainty these have resulted in. The effect of a mix of old and new identities in a context of social change is to produce more uncertainty.

In the British context this uncertainty expresses itself in patterns of both continuity and change. For example, there is evidence of changing 'ethnic' patterns in relation to a diverse mix of levels of educational attainment, the adoption of new 'mixed' or hybrid identities, and the emergence of cultural forms that draw on a range of heritages. Alongside these examples of change, other evidence indicates a continuity of patterns of exclusion in relation to racist violence, to pay levels and the opportunity for employment in senior posts. Both 'new' and 'old' trends point to some of the ways in which the 'ethnic' patterns produced by processes of racialization and ethnicization are part of the social structure of the UK, and this structure affects our identities. Social *structures* constrain people's ability to adopt certain identities. However, because there is also social *change* affecting the shape of these structures, opportunities are opened for people to adopt new or hybrid identities.

We can see then that in the changing times in which we live there is both uncertainty about, and diversity in, identity in relation to gender, the workplace, 'ethnicities' and nation. These changing times have also resulted in heated debates over the terminology of 'race' and 'ethnicity' and this has led to some people being diffident about discussing 'race' and racism because they fear 'saying the wrong thing'. It is particularly those from the white 'ethnic majority' who express this uncertainty. However, as we have seen, uncertainty about identities affects us all. This is the point made by Stuart Hall when he writes about his own shifting identity.

> I never called myself black because no one in the Caribbean did then. I've come home to an identity I was never allowed to settle for; discovering I've become something I was all the time: a black intellectual, a migrant ... People who are 68 should feel the ground solid under their feet. But I'm not surprised it feels shifting; ... More and more people feel life in this way.
>
> (Hall, quoted in Jaggi, 2000, p.9)

This experience of unsettled identities is then a condition shared by many of us in contemporary times. It is a feature that crosses 'ethnic' boundaries. We can extend a point made earlier in this chapter and in Chapter 1 (see the comment to Activity 1.3): difference is relational. To be different from some involves being the same as some others. Yet, what we are seeing here is that sameness may be shared across boundaries of difference. Sameness can underpin difference. One sociologist who has attempted to analyse the interconnection between sameness and difference is Avtar Brah (1996) who suggests that our identities are interconnected. She argues that it is important to pay attention to differences between people and also to the things they have in common across boundaries constructed on the basis of 'race', gender, social class and sexuality.

The idea that 'ethnic' differences and identities are constructed in a shared context of insecurity and uncertainty could be seen as an indication that there are no inequalities among various 'ethnic' groups. However, patterns and opportunities across 'ethnic' groups have profound ties to social inequalities. For example, racist violence produces a form of inequality, as do unequal pay levels and employment opportunities. In this sense the formation of ethnicized and racialized boundaries occurs in a context of inequalities.

SUMMARY

- Racialized and ethnicized identities are formed in a context of uncertainty.
- Uncertainty is a condition experienced by people across racialized and ethnicized boundaries.
- The racialized and ethnicized structure of the contemporary UK is characterized by both continuity and change.
- This structure is one of social inequality.

4 EXPANDING THE FIELD OF 'ETHNICITY'

In our discussion so far, each of the three questions noted in Chapter 1 and running throughout this book has been considered. In connection to the question about how identities are formed we have discussed the formation of identities for individuals and groups in relation to processes of racialization and ethnicization. The focus has been on people who are commonly identified as *minorities* on the basis of purported 'racial' or 'ethnic' characteristics. You have seen how being positioned as 'minority' is less to do with numbers in the population and more to do with social meanings and practices. You have also seen how the formation of an 'ethnic' or 'racial' identity arises in the context of how we see ourselves and how others see us. Or to put it in social scientific terms: it arises from the interaction between identities that we *adopt* and identities *ascribed* to us on the basis of things 'read off' from us. Understanding that 'racial' and 'ethnic' identities are formed in the interaction between how we see ourselves and how we are seen, enables us to grasp the complexity of this process. This is, firstly, because it shows that despite being a relational process, categorization of people into distinct groups is assumed to be natural and normal. Secondly, understanding the formation of identities in this way shows how the taken-for-granted or assumed naturalness of the categories of 'race' and 'ethnicity' masks the inequalities of power associated with these different categories.

This complexity also connects to the second question running through the chapters in this book. To what extent can we shape our own identities? Asking this question points to the impact of social structures on identity formation. Chapters 2 and 3 have shown that discussions of gender and class should be thought of as aspects of the structure of society. Our discussions so far show that 'ethnicity' should also be thought of as part of the social structure. The 'ethnic' diversity of the contemporary UK is part of its structure: it is one of the features that characterizes its current 'shape'. But this 'shape' is produced by social processes in which 'racial' and 'ethnic' differences and identities are constructed. It is in the tension between structure and process that people are able to take up, negotiate or redefine their identities as members of 'racial' or 'ethnic' groups.

SUMMARY

- Negotiations and redefinitions of racialized and ethnicized identities involve attempts to provide certainty about our own and others' 'racial' or 'ethnic' identity.

- This certainty is achieved by attributing meanings to particular forms of physical and cultural variation among human beings.

- The dynamics of identity formation vary according to the situation and context.

4.1 Whiteness as a racialized identity

In the preceding sections we have seen that the idea of 'racial' and 'ethnic' identities tends to be reserved for particular groups of people and that those defined as white are not explicitly identified in terms of 'racial' or 'ethnic' markers or categories. In contrast to this common assumption we suggest that *everybody* should be thought of as having an 'ethnicity'. This means that in societies characterized by racialized and ethnicized differences white people would also be thought of as 'marked' by 'racial' or 'ethnic' characteristics. When social scientists analyse processes of racialization and ethnicization they often concentrate on those positioned as less powerful and as 'minorities'. But if all identities are relational and everyone in the contemporary UK should be thought of as having an 'ethnicity', it is equally important to analyse the processes by which some groups are positioned as more powerful.

We can begin to explore some of the ways this occurs by looking at the following headline taken from *The Observer* (15 September 1996).

Ethnic winners outshine whites

This appeared as the heading to an article reporting on some findings of a Policy Studies Institute survey (Modood *et al.*, 1997) into the social and economic patterns found among the UK's 'minority ethnic' population. The article considers the existence of racism alongside changes in the place of people from different 'minority ethnic' groups in the social structure. It compared the relative performance of these groups in, for example, educational attainment, the labour market, housing and health. However, the headline positions white people as if they are outside of 'ethnic' categorization and without 'ethnicity'. This is achieved by the simple juxtaposition of the phrase 'ethnic winners' alongside but in opposition to 'whites'. This is a common practice.

[handwritten margin note: keeping the racialization ethnicity of whites separate from ethnic (social construction)]

Can you think of any similar examples? One example that we thought of was how usual it is for the print and broadcast media to talk of 'the ethnic communities' when they are referring to people of South Asian, African, African-Caribbean and other 'minority ethnic' people. Another was the labelling by supermarkets of some items as 'ethnic foods'.

The following example is a headline from the *Daily Mail* (13 December 2002).

Ethnic groups account for $4\frac{1}{2}$m Britons

This practice is common not only in news media and other forms of popular writing but is also prevalent in government publications. Another example can be found in the White Paper on Immigration, Nationality and Asylum that formed the basis of new legislation (applying to the UK) on these issues in 2002. You may note that sometimes people equate the UK with Britain and British with English. The UK is England, Northern Ireland, Scotland and Wales and Great Britain (often shortened to Britain) is the UK without Northern Ireland.

SECURE BORDERS, SAFE HAVEN: INTEGRATION WITH DIVERSITY IN MODERN BRITAIN

It was, ... accepted by the government that among many ethnic groups there was a continuing desire for parents to choose someone of a similar cultural background as partners for their children. As time goes on, we expect the number of arranged marriages between UK children and those living abroad to decline. Instead parents will seek to choose a suitable partner for their children from among their own communities in this country.

While embracing the diverse nature of our society, there are certain norms in relation to marriage in this country which we recognize as acceptable. For example, a marital partnership should be formed of only one man and one woman – we do not recognize polygamous households. Neither will we tolerate forced marriages. A man, or a woman must be free to decide whether to enter into marriage.

(Home Office, 2002, p.99)

These examples from *The Observer* and a government White Paper illustrate further some of the processes by which identities are formed. They point to the different processes taking place as people are positioned – or position themselves – in the social world. Let us take a moment to think about how these two examples illustrate this process.

1   There is a clear identification of 'ethnicity' or 'ethnic' group membership with black and Asian as opposed to white people: 'Ethnic winners outshine whites' and 'the government [accepted] that among many ethnic groups'.

2   The government White Paper connects 'ethnic' difference with certain ways of establishing marriage partnerships and households.

3   This identification of particular ways of organizing marriage and household formation is linked to a construction of the nation. Not only are certain forms of marriage and household positioned as outside the cultural norms of 'this country' but so too are marriage unions formed across the borders of the state expected to decline.

4   Without the extract saying so, we know that the White Paper example is focused on 'Asians' and that 'whites' are the norm against which they are being measured.

Both the newspaper and government examples show that 'ethnic' boundaries between white people and others are socially constructed. The White Paper example also shows that particular kinds of social practice are positioned as outside the cultural norms of the UK and of whiteness. Here, British national identity merges with whiteness as if it is only possible to be white and British. We can also use this example to elaborate on some of the points discussed in relation to the passport example in Chapter 1. Now, we can see that ethnicized difference can be socially constructed among those who may have shared access to a particular passport. The divide between 'us' and 'them' here is not exemplified by different passports and having rights in the UK state, but rather between persons who may be connected by the passports they hold but divided by the ways in which they organize

State
The cluster of institutions which claim ultimate law-making authority over a territory, and claim the monopoly on legitimate use of coercion and violence.

FIGURE 4.3   United by nationality, divided by ethnicization. Having the same passport does not guarantee equality

Nation
A named people who acknowledge aspects of a shared identity, laying claim to shared culture, history and territorial homeland.

Nation-state
A state which possesses external fixed, known, demarcated borders and has an internal uniformity of rule. People living within a nation-state do not necessarily constitute a single community.

marriages. As such, the invitation to identify with the **nation** as a cultural entity is on the basis of a particular kind of social practice not a particular nationality or of belonging to a **nation-state**.

SUMMARY

- White identities are ethnicized and racialized identities.
- Whiteness is part of the ethnicized social structure.
- Whiteness tends to be positioned outside this structure.
- Whiteness is used as an invisible marker against which other 'ethnicities' are judged.

In the rest of this section we want to explore some of the meanings of 'whiteness'. We will look at:

- How whiteness is an ethnicized category.
- Some of the ways that whiteness subsumes diverse 'ethnicities' that are hidden within it.
- Explore an example that opens up the category of whiteness and reveals a group subsumed within it.

Before going on to look at these issues stop for moment and think about what 'whiteness' means to you and make a note of the factors influencing your understanding of whiteness. For example, your racialized or ethnicized identity; your family history and 'ethnic' origins; whether you have a religious identity that influences your ideas.

4.1.1 Marking the 'unmarked'

How do we know about different 'ethnic' identities? What is the evidence? The period from the mid 1970s onwards saw a growing concern to collect statistical data on the patterns, experiences, attitudes and achievements among those parts of the population defined as belonging to 'minority ethnic' groups. As the perceived need for such statistics grew so too did the uses to which they could be put. It was felt that they provided some measure of discrimination and underachievement and that they could help in the identification of specific welfare and other social need. In Section 2.2, we noted that one suggested reason for the rejection of an inclusive definition of 'black' was that it resulted in public authorities failing to recognize the specific needs of Asian groups. Since the trend to collect 'ethnic' statistics began (in the 1970s), the collection of statistics in relation to 'race' and 'ethnicity' has become increasingly widespread and sophisticated.

Look at Box 4.1 (overleaf) showing the changing categories under which data relating to country of origin, 'ethnicity' and nationality were collected.

This listing makes it clear that the number of 'ethnic' group categories for 'ethnic minority' groups expanded in 1991 and 2001. However, the 'white' group remained singular until 2001. Until the white category was expanded, many people of differing 'ethnicities' encompassed within this 'racial' category were rendered invisible. For example, white Irish or Jewish people are among those who are made invisible by the undifferentiated category 'white'.

Stop for moment and consider the extent to which you think that the sub-divisions introduced into the category 'white' in the 2001 census resolves the issue of invisibility.

Although the 2001 census represents an attempt to put the category 'white' into a system of 'ethnic' classification this is not something that has been welcomed by all. It is seen by some people as creating problems. It is a moment when Englishness might be seen to be under threat from a variety of sources. There is greater uncertainty about what it means to be English when devolution and the recent resurgence of nationalism among the nations that make up the UK have challenged what it means to be English

BOX 4.1   Changing census categories: the shifting 'ethnic' question

1971

There were three questions in this year. They were used to estimate the 'size of the population of New Commonwealth and Pakistan ethnic origin' (Office of Population Censuses and Surveys, 1981, p.10).

(i) Country of Birth
(ii) Country of Birth of Father
(iii) Country of Birth of Mother.

1981

There was only one question in this year.

(i) Country of Birth

The decision to limit the question relating to nationality, national origin and 'ethnic' group membership followed a lengthy period of testing and consultation. This period of testing and consultation did not involve much discussion about the category 'white' and the groups included within it.

1991

In this census two questions provided the main source of data on national origin, country of birth, and 'ethnic' group membership.

(i) Country of Origin
(ii) Ethnic Group. This was sub-divided into:

- White
- Black-Caribbean
- Black African
- Black Other
- Indian
- Pakistani
- Bangladeshi
- Chinese
- Other Groups
  - Asian
  - Other.

(Office of Population Censuses and Surveys, 1991)

2001

In this census there was one question but it offered a wider range of responses. The 'white' category was sub-divided as shown below and there was a whole sub-set of categories under the heading 'mixed'.

What is your ethnic group?

Choose one section from (a) to (e) then tick the appropriate box to indicate your cultural background.

(a) White
- ☐ British
- ☐ Irish
- ☐ Any other White background. *Please write in below*

  ....

(b) Mixed
- ☐ White and Black Caribbean
- ☐ White and Black African
- ☐ White and Asian
- ☐ Any other mixed background. *Please write in below*

  ....

(c) Asian or Asian British
- ☐ Indian
- ☐ Pakistani
- ☐ Bangladeshi
- ☐ Any other Asian background. *Please write in below*

  ....

(d) Black or Black British
- ☐ Caribbean
- ☐ African
- ☐ Any other Black background. *Please write in below*

  ....

(e) Chinese or Other ethnic group
- ☐ Chinese
- ☐ Any other. *Please write in below*

  ....

(Office for National Statistics, 1999)

and the status of being British. In this way simply expanding the 'white' category to include 'British', 'Irish', 'Any other' may not resolve the issue of visibility of white Scots or Welsh in a way that seems equitable to those claiming such an identity. Similarly, Scots, Welsh and other European 'ethnicities' are left out of the 'Mixed' categories listed in the 2001 census. The only space for them being in the 'Any other' category at the end of the list of options.

ACTIVITY 4.4

Read through the following extract taken from *The Mail on Sunday* (10 March 2002) and make notes on the following questions.

- What does the author of the article mean by English?

- How does the author position 'the English'?

- What evidence is there that the author thinks that to be assigned an 'ethnic' status is denigrating and offensive?

- What evidence is there that the author sees 'English' and 'black' as categories and identities that cannot be combined?

Government relegates English to 'wild card' ethnic status, with Gipsies and Kosovars

by Simon Walters (Political Editor)

Tony Blair faced a race row last night after it was revealed that a new Government drive to check the ethnic background of the population gives the 'English' the same status as Gipsies, Kosovars and Irish travellers.

Ethnic coding forms to monitor NHS patients, schoolchildren, benefit claimants and crime victims define English as a 'wild card' category, among 47 racial minorities. ...

The changes, which follow reforms in the 1976 Race Relations Act, affect everyone who works in or uses any public service – schools, police, town halls, hospitals – virtually the entire population.

Children will be asked to say which racial group they think they belong to, and will not be automatically put in the same group as their parents.

The new ethnic monitoring survey has been introduced in recent months but does not take full effect until May. The new law forces authorities to use the results to draw up new anti-discrimination programmes.

Health department documents say the aims include targeting special help for the high number of 'obese black Caribbean and Pakistani women, Bangladeshis suffering from psychiatric illness, black Caribbean men affected by strokes and Irish women with heart disease.'

The survey goes much further than last year's controversial census which asked people to pick from one of 16 main race groupings, including British, Any Other White, Asian, Chinese, Indian, Pakistani and Black, while excluding English. The new version includes the same 16 groups, but this time, local officials are allowed to 'pick 'n' mix' to extend the questionnaire to cover 47 'wild card' categories, depending on their area.

These 'optional extras' include English, along with Irish Traveller, Gipsy/Romany, Kosovar, Somali, Welsh, Serbian, and even Cornish, the only county to be given its own 'ethnic' title.

'We are a coalition of minorities'

English is officially defined as a subgroup of 'Any Other White'.

Tory frontbencher Liam Fox said last night: 'This survey is further proof that the Labour Government sees us not as one country but as a coalition of minorities.'

'It is the worst possible fragmentation of society. To treat English people as the same ethnic grouping as Gipsies is deeply insulting.'

And this is how we are pigeon-holed in the 'ethnicity' test

New 'ethnicity' tests force NHS, police and town hall chiefs to find out which of 16 racial groupings staff, patients, crime victims, pupils and others belong to.

The categories are: British, Irish, Any other White background, White and Black Caribbean, White and Black African, White and Asian, Any other mixed background, Indian, Pakistani, Bangladeshi, Any other Asian background, Caribbean, African, Any other Black background, Chinese, Any other ethnic group. Local officials can pick from an additional 47 'wild card' ethnic categories. They are:

White Group
English, Scottish, Welsh, Northern Irish, Cornish, Cypriot, Greek, Greek Cypriot, Turkish, Turkish Cypriot, Italian, Irish Traveller, Gipsy/Romany, Polish, All republics from the former USSR, Kosovar, Albanian, Bosnian, Croatian, Serbian, Other republics from the former Yugoslavia, Mixed white, Other white European, European unspecified, European mixed.

Mixed Groups
Black and Asian, Black and Chinese, Black and White, Chinese and White, Asian and Chinese.

Asian or Asian British Group
Mixed Asian, Punjabi, Kashmiri, East African Asian, Sri Lankan, Tamil, Sinhalese, British Asian, Caribbean Asian.

Black or Black British Group
Somali, Mixed Black, Nigerian, Black British.

Other Ethnic Groups
Chinese, Vietnamese, Japanese, Filipino, Malaysian.

Source: Walters, 2002

C O M M E N T

Some of the first clues to the answers to these questions are to be found in the main and sub-headings of the article. These claim that 'English' has been relegated to '"wild card" ethnic status' and that 'we' are to be pigeon-holed in an '"ethnicity" test'. The tone of outrage suggests that designation of 'we', the English, as an 'ethnic' group is denigrating and offensive. This outrage is indicated further in the first two paragraphs where categorization of 'the English' in ways similar to 'Gipsies, Kosovars and Irish Travellers', or as one group among a range of 'racial' minorities is presented as both insulting and ludicrous. In this the author implicitly positions 'the English' as falling outside any rational system of 'ethnic' classification.

He also implicitly counterpoises Englishness and 'non-whiteness' by the way in which he argues his opposition to the proposed uses of a wide range of categories. For example, he refers to '47 "wild card" categories', the inclusion of 'English' as an 'optional extra', and that 'English is officially defined as a sub-group of "Any Other White"'. Finally, the connotation of 'English' as 'white' and 'normal' is evident in statements about the use of the widened array of 'ethnic' categories for the identification of specific needs (termed 'special help') of 'black Caribbean and Pakistani women, Bangladeshis ... , black Caribbean men ... and Irish women ... '.

The article contains many additional points. This is especially so in relation to the way that the category 'white' hides within it diverse but subordinate 'ethnicities' and how it links constructions of racialized and ethnicized difference and national identity. It illustrates that for some people 'ethnicity' is not something that can be attached to being English, and that 'English' is equated with white in a taken-for-granted way. This identification of Englishness and Britishness with whiteness and the representation of both of these as being under threat has accompanied the increasingly multicultural character of many of the UK's urban centres. Politicians such as Peter Griffiths and Enoch Powell in the 1960s, Margaret Thatcher in the 1970s and David Blunkett in 2002 have, at times, used phrases such as 'nigger neighbour', 'rivers of blood', and 'swamping' to construct the presence of people with different national, 'ethnic' or 'racial' origins as dangerous for the 'majority ethnic' population. Sarah Neal (2002) has made the point that this is linked to an identification of England/UK as a white space. She also shows how depictions of the countryside are used to support such constructions. For example, she quotes the following, taken from an editorial in a newspaper from the Isles of Scilly.

> The beauty of our countryside is testament to millennia of careful husbandry, from which a community life developed. Not an urban, multicultural way of life, but the heritage of ethnic Britons – with roots going back 2,500 years ... Farmers and their supporters are not members of powerful Trade Unions (sic) and have not – until now – threatened to march on Parliament. *Ninety-nine-point-nine per cent of farmers are white, law abiding and Christian.*
>
> (*Tresco Times*, Spring 2001, cited in Neal, 2002, p.446, emphasis in original)

Now think back to the article from *The Mail on Sunday* in Activity 4.4. What similarities and differences can you see between that article and the extract from the *Tresco Times* in their approach to Britishness, whiteness and multiculturalism?

We can discern many commonalities between the two articles. For example, the way in which they implicitly associate Britishness with whiteness and counterpoise both against multiculturalism. There is, however, one significant difference between the two articles. In the latter one 'ethnicity' is used as the ground upon which to situate and distinguish Britishness.

A Briton is a member of a distinct 'ethnic' group with a very long heritage and has a commitment to a peaceable and law-abiding way of life. It is also a way of life that is essentially rural. This claim to an 'ethnic' status for British people differentiates it from the earlier piece despite the fact that they share a common concern.

FIGURE 4.4   The 'Liberty & Livelihood' march

This appears to be a British **nationalism** based on 'ethnic' nationalism. However, as Benedict Anderson has argued, the idea of a 'nation' is *imagined*. He uses the notion of an *imagined community* to explain how, although

> even the members of the smallest nation will never know most of their fellow members, meet them, or ever hear of them ... The nation is imagined as limited because even the largest of them, encompassing perhaps a billion human beings, has finite, if elastic boundaries, beyond which lie other nations ... it is the imagined community because, regardless of the actual inequality and exploitation that may prevail ... the nation is always conceived as a deep horizontal comradeship.
>
> (Anderson, 1983, pp.15–16)

The second piece also illustrates further the relational character of 'ethnic' groups and identities. Thus 'ethnic Britons' are constructed as different from, but in relation to, those with an urban, multicultural way of life. This is not, however, the end of the story as identifying 'Britons' in 'ethnic' terms has another effect because it implicitly suggests that all those with a different

Nationalism
The emotive identification with a nation and what is seen to be its political project.

'ethnicity' and heritage cannot be included as being truly British even if they are born on British soil. In this way whiteness, even though redefined in terms of 'ethnicity', is reinstated as authentic Britishness.

We can also see evidence of the effect of uncertainty on the process of identity formation in this short extract from the *Tresco Times*. In its claim for the longevity of British rural ways of life we can read this extract as evidence of the adoption of an identity as a protection from the uncertainty represented by wide patterns of social change.

FIGURE 4.5   Unsettling Britishness?

SUMMARY

- Over the last 30 years there has been a proliferation of 'ethnic' categories for particular groups.
- The category 'white' has not undergone the same degree of division into distinct 'ethnic' categories.
- There has been both resistance to, and a claim for, the designation of 'English' and 'British' as 'ethnic' identities.
- Both opposition to, and claims for, a designation as 'ethnic' have been used in an attempt to reinstate whiteness as the dominant and normative identity.

4.2 Opening up the category 'white': the 'ethnic' claims of the Irish

As we have seen, these attempts to reassert the centrality of whiteness are linked to the uncertainties that have accompanied recent processes of economic and social change. The proliferation of 'ethnic' groups through processes of ethnicization has at times been greeted with resentment. Social scientists have increasingly begun to turn their attention to exploring how whiteness is reproduced as a dominant category and the effect this has on those encompassed within it. This has included how some are made invisible and subordinate. Some Irish people have been particularly influential in this process.

Since the 1980s, Irish community organizations in places such as Sheffield, Manchester, Glasgow, Birmingham and London have been campaigning for recognition as a specific 'ethnic' group. In large part the impetus for this has been evidence showing the extent of discriminatory treatment experienced by Irish people as they deal with public and private agencies. Because of the growing evidence of such practices, the Commission for Racial Equality sponsored some research into the extent of such discrimination and its influence on the experiences of Irish people (Hickman and Walter, 1997).

ACTIVITY 4.5

A short extract from this report is reproduced here. Read it and make a note of how dominant constructions of whiteness affect the Irish.

CONSTRUCTIONS OF WHITENESS AND THE INVISIBILITY OF THE IRISH

Because of the myth of homogeneity and the assumption that all whites share the same ethnicity, ... [it is believed] there is no basis upon which someone who is white is disadvantaged on 'ethnic' grounds or can be subject to racism, claims to the contrary by the Irish are greeted with incredulity or hostility. The demands made by Irish community groups for a culturally sensitive service for Irish people are a direct challenge to these constructions of whiteness. ...

A number of Irish groups in different contexts explained their anxiety that assessments of clients and their needs were made by professionals who assumed that there was no need to take into account any specific circumstances when dealing with an Irish person because of their whiteness.

(Hickman and Walter, 1997, p.107)

C O M M E N T

The report claims that dominant constructions of whiteness mean that racism against the Irish is not believed and that the specific needs of Irish people using public services are rendered invisible and therefore not met.

This example of the claim to a specific 'ethnicity' by some Irish community organizations and individuals echoes the claims we noted earlier by Asian people dissatisfied with the all-embracing use of the term 'black'. The concerns of both Irish and South Asian groups illustrate ways in which claims to racialized and ethnicized identities can be linked to attempts to challenge social inequalities. Firstly, both have challenged their invisibility within categories that assumed or imposed shared 'racial' or 'ethnic' identities. Secondly, both have linked their adoption of an 'ethnic' identity to a demand for access to resources and better treatment by service providers, especially those in the public sector. Yet, in the wider social structure, Irish people are often positioned in similar ways to people identified as Bangladeshi, Pakistani and African Caribbean. A feature they share is relative disadvantage in relation to a number of social indicators, such as ill health and poor housing conditions.

Whilst not all those claiming an Irish identity are white, both social science research on the Irish in Britain and the evidence obtained by Irish community organizations shows that the term 'white' should not be seen as homogeneous and monolithic. Failure to open up the category 'white' has obscured the diverse 'ethnicities' within it. This, in its turn, obscures the hierarchies and differential power relations among those 'ethnicities' encompassed within the category 'white'.

SUMMARY

- Claims made by Irish individuals and groups have contributed to the category 'white' becoming subject to critique and analysis.
- This has revealed the subordinations and inequalities among different 'ethnic' groups hidden within the category 'white'.
- This attempt to open up the category has been linked to a claim for specific services.

5 CONCLUSION

In drawing this chapter to a conclusion we can return to the three questions that run throughout the book and think about how they connect to a consideration of racialized and ethnicized identities. We have argued that, as with all identities, racialized and ethnicized identities are formed relationally, that is by making a claim of similarity with some and a claim of difference from others. We have shown that racialized and ethnicized identities are formed in the context of different types of inequality, which could include, for example, employment, education or housing, but also in terms of what is claimed as truly or fully British. Power inequalities are evident in such claims in that it is the white 'majority ethnic' group that has the power to define who is to be included and who excluded from fully belonging to the nation. We have also shown that identities are not fixed but shift in changing contexts. Collective action, as in the Black Power and black consciousness movements, may contribute to the development of these changing contexts and open the space for more diverse new 'racial' and 'ethnic' identities to arise. Racialized and ethnicized identities may also be formed in the context of struggles to gain access to resources and for social recognition. We have seen this in relation to some 'minority ethnic' groups. For the 'majority ethnic' group new 'racial' or 'ethnic' identities have been formed in a struggle to claim 'authentic' Britishness/Englishness and dominance within the social structure.

However, we have also shown that while changes in the social structure may open up spaces for a redefinition of identities, these structures also act as a constraint on this process. This was illustrated by the idea of 'new times and old times'. Racialized and ethnicized identities are thus formed in a complex interplay between social structures and individual and collective agency.

Finally, we have shown how shifts in, and struggles over, 'racial', 'ethnic' and national identities occur in a context of change and uncertainty. This uncertainty is at a global and national level as well as at the level of specific localities. It occurs in relation to other aspects of people's lives. For example, the opportunities for employment or access to public resources; the struggle for respect and recognition; changes in what it means to be a man or woman; what it means to be black or white, Indian, African, Scottish or Irish in the contemporary UK. All these may produce uncertainty. In this context racialized and ethnicized identities – whether ascribed or adopted – can be seen as one way in which people attempt to cope with change.

Mercer, K. (1990) 'Welcome to the jungle' in Rutherford, J. (ed.) *Identity, Community, Culture, Difference*, London, Lawrence and Wishart.

Modood, T., Berthoud, R., Lakey, J., Nazroo, J., Smith, P., Virdee, S. and Beishon, S. (1997) *Ethnic Minorities in Britain: Diversity and Disadvantage*, London, Policy Studies Institute.

Neal, S. (2002) 'Rural landscapes, representations and racism: examining multicultural citizenship and policy-making in the English countryside', *Ethnic and Racial Studies,* vol.25, no.3, pp.442–61.

Office for National Statistics (1999) *The 2001 Census of Population*, Cmnd. 4253, London, The Stationery Office for Office for National Statistics.

Office of Population Censuses and Surveys (1981, 1991) *Guide to the Census Questions*, London, HMSO.

The Stationery Office (1999) *Report of an Inquiry by Sir William Macpherson of Cluny: The Stephen Lawrence Inquiry*, London, The Stationery Office (Cm. 4262).

Walters, S. (2002) 'Government relegates English to "wild card" ethnic status, with Gipsies and Kosovars', *The Mail on Sunday*, 10 March, p.11.

Webster, W. (1998) *Imagining Home: Gender, 'Race' and National Identity, 1945–64*, London, UCL Press.

Younge, G. (2002) 'At ease with our diversity', *The Guardian*, 13 May.

FURTHER READING

Paula Rothenberg (2000) *Invisible Privilege*, Lawrence, Kansas, University of Kansas Press. This book is a personal narrative of the author's autobiography as a white US, middle-class Jewish woman who is an academic. It presents an accessible analysis of how everyday life (including higher education) is marked by 'race', class, and gender bias in ways that makes these inequalities invisible. Rothenberg uses her own experiences to analyse how white people's belief in their own good intentions often blinds them to their societal privilege and their role in perpetuating inequality. She argues that people across constructed identity boundaries can 'ask each other's questions' and use privilege constructively. For example, men can sometimes be particularly effective in critiquing sexism and white people can raise the question of racism.

Glenn Jordan and Chris Weedon (1995) *Cultural Politics: Class, Gender, Race and the Postmodern World*, Oxford, Blackwell, Chapter 9, 'Marking difference, asserting power: the cultural politics of racism'. This chapter from Jordan and Weedon's book provides a useful discussion of the relationship between forms of racism and the development of identities across boundaries of difference. It uses historical and contemporary material to present an accessible discussion of some of the ways that racism constructs the identities of racialized groups and although the focus is mainly on black people in the UK and the USA it has some discussion of white people and other racialized groups. One point to note is that Jordan and Weedon use the terms 'subjectivity' and 'identity' interchangeably but in ways that you will find familiar.

Afterword

Kath Woodward

This book has, as it promised, been question led. In the 'Introduction' I posed three framing questions. The discussion has addressed these questions by focusing on the contributions of different social scientists, whose responses have in themselves generated more questions. How do we make sense of ourselves as individuals in relation to the social world which we inhabit? When the world changes do we remain constant or does who we are change too and how does this happen?

Now I want to return to my framing questions, starting with the first one: *how are identities formed?*

The processes involved in taking up identities require some connections between individuals and the world in which they live. We have to be recruited into an identity, which involves some kind of active engagement on our part. Do you remember the football example in Chapter 1? More importantly, as was argued in Chapter 4, there are points in time when people identify with the nation and actively take up a national identity. How are we recruited into these identities? One important aspect of the process is the way in which people represent themselves and recognize others. We use symbols, such as language, clothes, flags, badges, to mark ourselves as having the same identity as one group of people and a different identity from the others.

Identity is always in some way marked by difference and sameness. Identity relies upon individuals' understanding of these symbolic markers, whether of gender categories, or class identity, or racialized or ethnicized identities. Differences may be stereotyped and involve an exaggerated selection of defining characteristics or, as we saw with the fuzzy gender categories in Chapter 2, they may be much more complex and subtle, as well as involving contradiction and conflict. In order to identify with an identity position we have to be able to imagine ourselves as occupying that position; that is, to think of ourselves, in our heads, as British or Irish, as the good mother, the successful career person, as streetwise, as female or as male. As we saw in Chapter 2, the process of forming a gender identity is not only influenced by our biology. Children have to understand the categories through which their own society classifies femininity and masculinity and to pick up the appropriate clues. Legal categories such as those of ethnicity included in the collection of official data such as the census, both reflect change, as the categories change as they did between the 1991 and 2001 censuses, but also create limitations upon how we categorize ourselves.

Sometimes the process of recruitment might even be unconscious. We may not be fully aware of why we appear to have embraced a particular identity.

The process of identification is complex and can involve the operation of factors which are part of our own personal histories, such as early childhood experience. At times there may be a moment of recognition in the identification process, where we may not be quite sure why we think 'that's me', but it just seems right. The concept of interpellation offers some insight into what is going on when people recognize themselves; for example, in advertisements or in political recruiting material.

Many of the approaches which have been explored in this book have emphasized the social aspects of the identity equation. Although as individuals we have to identify – that is, to take up an identity actively – there are also structures in the social world with which we identify. Some structures, picked out in Chapter 1, were explored in more detail in the following chapters. Gender is an important aspect of identity. Even very young children need to know whether they are a girl or a boy. Gender categories are constructed through our biological bodies and through social and cultural classificatory systems. At some points in history, class identity has been very important. These identities involve individuals recognizing their own class position and having some degree of class consciousness, which is also acknowledged by others. Traditional views of identity, including the Marxist and Weberian approaches to class, have emphasized the role of social structures in shaping people's identities. More recent approaches have stressed the interaction between the social and the personal, such as when individuals and groups negotiate their identities and represent themselves through patterns of consumption. Ethnicity and race are also social structures which influence the identities which people can adopt. However, these structures are changing and may be renegotiated. The constraints of racialized identities can also be challenged through collective action as Chapter 4 showed. Identities are not fixed; they are fluid and both individuals and social structures are changing.

How much scope is there for the negotiation of identities? Are we limited to a great extent by our bodies, by our economic circumstances, by the social construction and stereotypes of gender and ethnicity? Can people exercise some agency in the creation of their collective and individual identities?

This leads in to our next framing question about the relationship between agency and structure: *to what extent can we shape our own identities?*

I have argued that there has to be some active engagement on our part in taking up identities. However, as has been shown throughout the book, there are severe constraints on the degree of agency which we may be able to exercise. For example, economic circumstances, changes in employment, poverty, racism and lack of recognition of our ethnic or national identities all deny us access to identities which we might want to take up. Cultural construction of gender, social regulation and even legal categories and classifications prevent individuals from taking up alternative identities. Social attitudes towards ethnic diversity can limit its celebration by those who are constructed as outsiders. Our own bodies put limits on what it is possible to achieve. However, the interrelationship between the personal and the social involves negotiation. People reconstruct their own identities, even within the constraints of poverty. Through the collective action of social movements, of class-based action, and through asserting ethnic identities and national identities within a multi-ethnic UK, people reshape the social structures which restrict them. Even at the level of the individual, through body projects, it is possible to recreate our identities through transforming our bodies, by getting fit, by challenging stereotypes.

This leads to our third framing question: *are there more uncertainties about identity at this moment in the UK?*

The book has presented several examples of social change in the contemporary UK. Certainties about employment, especially male employment in manufacturing industry, about family life and gender roles, about being British and the ethnic and national composition of the UK itself have shifted in the period since the Second World War. There has been a move away from class-based identities and the security that might have been afforded by particular patterns of employment, the associated gendered roles within families and assumptions about what it means to be white. In one sense these changes can be seen as indicating greater uncertainty. Contemporary concerns with identity can be seen as focusing on presenting ourselves to others, through consuming identities, and through lifestyle and developing ourselves as individuals. This can be contrasted with the changing ways in which collective identities have been forged – for example, through class identification. New social movements have produced a new focus for the politics of collective identities, with their concerns with gender, sexuality and race, in some instances making 'the personal political'. Uncertainties can also be expressed as responses to change and the opportunities for diversity which are offered. In the twenty-first century there is a greater diversity of forms of domestic living than in the 1950s. Gender stereotypes are challenged by reconstructions and more fluid identities. The UK is a multi-ethnic society, albeit one which still manifests the constraints of racism. There is legislative as well as cultural recognition of the separate identities of Irish, Scottish and Welsh peoples within the UK. Uncertainty and diversity coexist.

This book has also been about social science knowledge and its production. We began with questions which we have revisited and to which we have added several more. This illustrates areas of the process of social science enquiry. We started with questions but quickly moved on to claims: claims about identity and how it was defined. In order to find out we looked at a variety of evidence. The book has offered a range of evidence, both quantitative and qualitative. One source of evidence which was cited in Chapter 1 involved a personal narrative, the testimony of an individual. This raised other questions about the need for additional evidence as well as the need to ask more questions about one person's account. What else could social science tell us? What were the social elements involved. We suggested class and gender at this point, and these are structures which Chapters 2 and 3 explored in more detail. Chapter 2 unpacked some of the meanings of gender and offered evidence of how ideas about gender identities are produced. Chapter 3 presented empirical evidence about the distribution of wealth, with some powerful representations of data; for example, in the income parade. In order to evaluate the evidence, we looked at different theoretical approaches within the social sciences. The inclusion of some factors – gender in Chapter 2 and class and economic factors in Chapter 3 – also highlights the exclusion of others. One of the important questions posed in evaluating the evidence involves asking what is missing. Where we come from, in particular, race and ethnicity, are key elements on making sense of who we are. Chapter 4's discussion of racialization and ethnicization and the ways in which meanings are produced about identity by placing it, in terms of time, history and place, adds another component to the circuit of our social science investigation of identity.

Throughout the book we have indicated some of the ways in which representation is a key component in linking the personal to the social. Meanings about gender, class and ethnicity are produced through their representation within culture. Children learn how to categorize through gendered representations of dress and behaviour. These symbolic systems are what we use in everyday interactions. This is how we categorize other people as being the same as us or as different from us. As we saw in Chapter 3, meanings about poverty and about what constitutes poverty are represented through culture, although those who experience it may challenge these representations, especially of being victims, and struggle to redefine themselves within these cultural as well as material constraints. Representations of race, especially of how others see us and of how we see ourselves, are produced through cultural processes. Sometimes meanings are unstated and assumed, as has been the case with whiteness, as if ethnicity were only a characteristic of black people.

We started with questions and have added several more to the initial framing three. We have suggested ways in which social scientists address these questions. We have offered some claims about identity and some ways of supporting and evaluating these claims. The book has addressed some of the important aspects of identity and indicated some of the complex ways in which identities are formed, stressing the importance of the interaction between the personal and the social. There are no simple answers. There are tensions between the personal and the social and between the agency people can exert and the constraints of social structures. There are uncertainties, which are historically specific. We live in changing times. We have multiple identities and identities are multifaceted. Multiple identities offer the possibility of diversity and have the potential for reconstruction and renewal. This is why identity matters.

Acknowledgements

Grateful acknowledgement is made to the following sources for permission to reproduce material in this book.

Chapter 1

Text

Kay, J. (1991) 'So you think I'm a mule?', *The Adoption Papers*, Sheba Feminist Publishers. Copyright © 1991 Jackie Kay.

Figures

Figure 1.1: examples of UK passports. Crown copyright is reproduced with the permission of the Controller of Her Majesty's Stationery Office; Figure 1.2: ICI Alkathene advert from *Ideal Home* magazine, August 1956. © The Advertising Archives; Figure 1.3: Mike Levers/The Open University; Figures 1.4 and 1.6: © Martin Jenkinson; Figure 1.5(top): Courtesy of Sheffield Wednesday Football Club. Kindly donated by W.E.A., South Yorkshire District; Figure 1.5(bottom): National Coal Board advertisement by kind permission of W.E.A., South Yorkshire District; Figure 1.7: © Nick Cobbing; Figures 1.8 and 1.9: Peter Marshall/Photofusion; Figure 1.10: Andi Faryl Schreiber/Format; Figure 1.11: Chris Barry; Figure 1.12: Copyright © Age Concern England.

Illustration

p.16: 'True self' by Chris Madden. Copyright © Paperlink Ltd, London 1999.

Chapter 2

Text

Blackadder II in *Blackadder: The Whole Damn Dynasty* (Michael Joseph, 1998) copyright © Richard Curtis and Ben Elton, 1985. From *The Blackadder* by Richard Curtis and Rowan Atkinson, Ben Elton and John Lloyd, copyright © 1998 by Richard Curtis, Rowan Atkinson, Ben Elton and John Lloyd. Used by permission of Penguin, a division of Penguin Group (USA) Inc.

Figures

Figure 2.1: Birth Certificate. © Crown Copyright. Published by permission of the Controller of Her Majesty's Stationery Office and the Office for National Statistics; Figure 2.2: Turner, P.J. (1995) *Sex, Gender and Identity*, The British Psychological Society; Figure 2.3: © Mike Levers/The Open University; Figure 2.5: Bright, M. (1998) 'Boys performing badly', *The Observer*, 4 January 1998. Copyright © *The Observer*; Figure 2.6: Kimura, D. (1992) 'Sex differences in the brain', *Scientific American*, September 1992. Courtesy of Jared Schneidman Design; Figure 2.8: © Hector Breeze. From *The Guardian*, 7 January 1998; Figure 2.9: Sally and Richard Greenhill; Figure 2.10: Mary

Index